Japanese Brush Painting Techniques

your sumi-e book is alive
excellent fresh.
I shall surely recommend your
book as one making life possible
Hurrah!

—Paul Reps

Japanese Brush Painting Techniques

Sumi-e
A Meditation in Ink

Paul Siudzinski

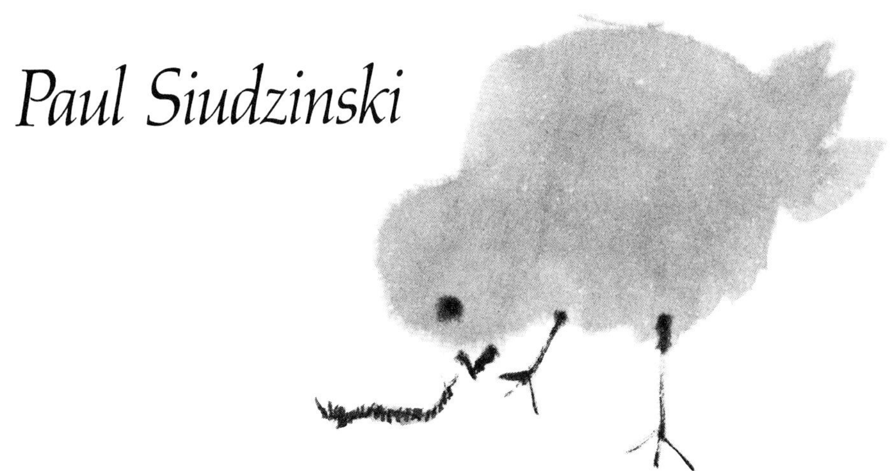

Sterling Publishing Co., Inc.   New York
Distributed in the U.K. by Blandford Press

To   Mara

The items in Figures 41 through 49 are from the collection of Steve Mindel of Kyoto, Japan.

Library of Congress Cataloging in Publication Data

Siudzinski, Paul.
    Japanese brush painting techniques.

    Previously published: Sumi-e. New York : Drake, 1978.
    1. Sumie.   2. Ink painting, Japanese—Technique.
3. Ink painting—Technique. I. Title.
ND2462.S58   1983   751.42′52   83-9107
ISBN 0-8069-7752-3 (pbk.)

© 1978 by Paul Siudzinski
Published in 1983 by Sterling Publishing Co., Inc.
Two Park Avenue, New York, N.Y. 10016
First published under the title "Sumi-e: A Meditation in Ink"
Distributed in Australia by Oak Tree Press Co., Ltd.
P.O. Box K514 Haymarket, Sydney 2000, N.S.W.
Distributed in the United Kingdom by Blandford Press
Link House, West Street, Poole, Dorset BH15 1LL, England
Distributed in Canada by Oak Tree Press Ltd.
℅ Canadian Manda Group, P.O. Box 920, Station U
Toronto, Ontario, Canada M8Z 5P9

CONTENTS

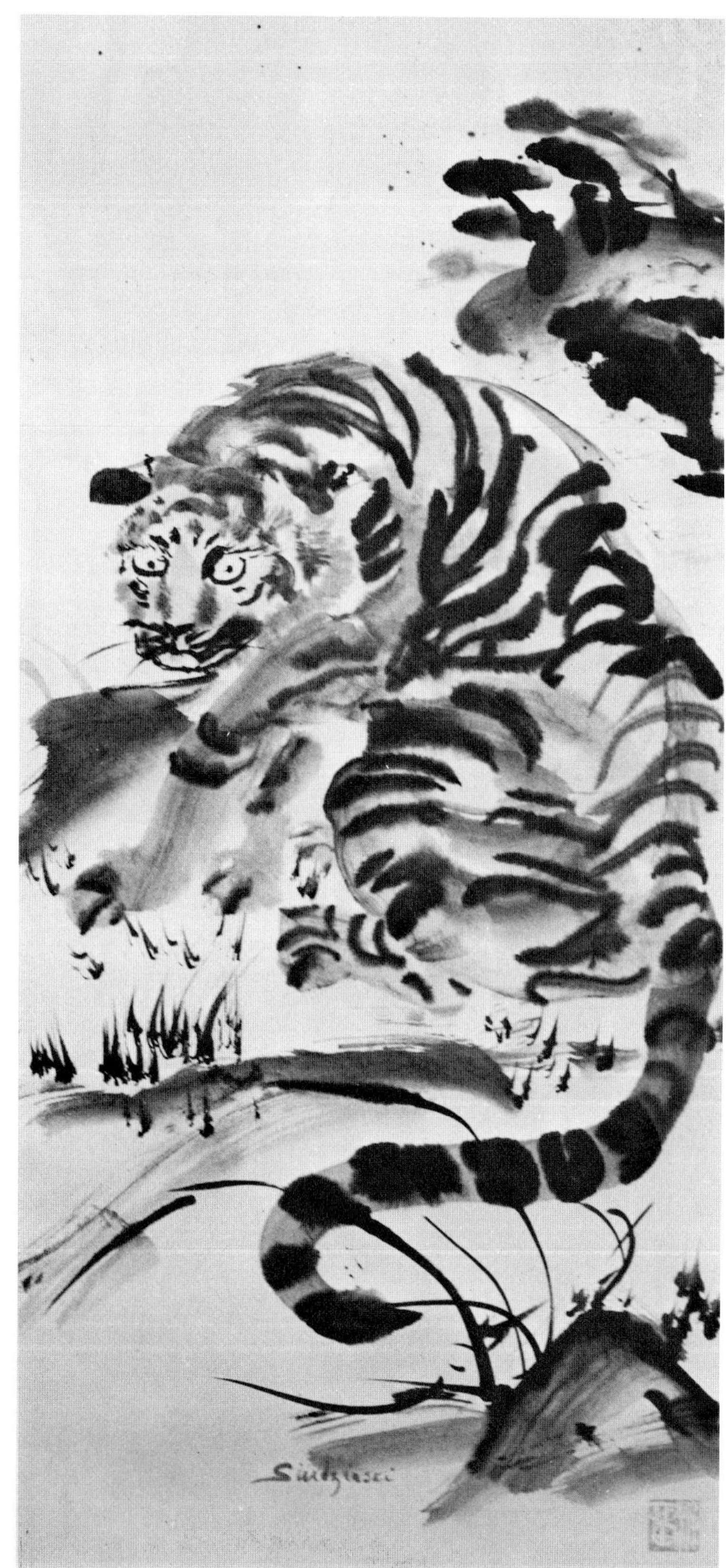

Dragon Fighter. The tiger is the only creature able to challenge the dragon, according to Japanese tradition. The two subjects are often portrayed in paired scrolls. This painting was done rapidly in an impressionistic style.

PREFACE

Sumi-e is a basic art form which uses only black ink, clear water, and white paper. Its materials are as simple as the elements of the universe, an empty space in which earth and water take their form. As nature captures the essence, mystery, and totality of the universe in each living thing, so, too, sumi-e captures the spirit of its subject in a few strokes. Its primary characteristics are simplicity, understatement, and clear expression; there is no overpainting, no exacting detail work, no repeated layering of colors. The only colors sumi-e employs are the infinite variety of subtle tones that result from the combination of black ink and clear water. The effect is always striking, elegant, and direct.

History of Sumi-e. Ink painting is an ancient Oriental art. Although its beginnings are found in early line drawing and calligraphy, what we call *suiboku-ga* (water-ink painting) was known in China as early as the seventh century. It was then that the rich variety of shadings we associate with sumi-e first appeared. There were two schools of ink painting in China, the Hakuju-ga, or Northern School, and the Nanju-ga, or Southern School. The Hakuju-ga painters first outlined the subject and then shaded it. The Nanju-ga painters used a *mokkotsu* (boneless) technique in which no outlines were used. A relatively wet, ink-laden brush is applied directly to the page to shape the forms of the subject. This book derives from this mokkotsu tradition.

Chinese *suiboku-ga* was first introduced to Japan by Zen monks during the latter half of the thirteenth century. But while the earliest influences were of the Northern School, later Zen painters were heavily influenced by the "boneless" Southern School. The Japanese artists soon created an independent style characterized by brevity, originality, spontaneity, and freedom of expression. Landscapes, Buddhist portrait paintings, and simple themes like birds or flowers became popular subjects.

Sumi-e has maintained through the centuries a loose affiliation with that search for enlightenment which the study of Zen implies. Zen emphasizes physical labor. Painting, too, is work, from the grinding of the ink to the mounting of the finished painting. The subjects of sumi-e — tea bowls, brooms, bamboo, birds — similarly remind one that enlightenment is found in the common things of life. And in the spontaneous nature of sumi-e is found a link to the sudden illumination sought by Zen practitioners.

Many schools of sumi-e developed in Japan over the centuries, some very precise and detailed, others spontaneous and charged with emotion and insight. The sumi-e described in this book is a spiritual descendent of the simplest and most direct kinds of Zen paintings. You will not learn here how to paint elaborate landscapes or portraits of Zen monks. *A Meditation in Ink* is intended to produce paintings that communicate directly the spontaneous, intuitive perception of the inner eye. Although it relies on the insights generated by meditative attentiveness, it is not a Zen meditation. It is a way of painting, where both "way" and "painting" are translated, in their broadest meanings, as a path of seeing.

How Can Painting Be a Meditation?   *A Meditation in Ink* is a constant process of paying attention. The basic premise here is that we can live life more fully if we pay attention to what is happening to us in the moment. Many of us spend much of our
time unaware of what we are doing. On one level we may know what we are "doing."
But in another sense, we are asleep to ourselves. Often we daydream, fantasize, or
carry on conversations in our heads. But meditation is a way to pay attention.

Sumi-e painting can be a form of meditation. In painting we have a specific task,
that of putting on paper what we see before us. *A Meditation in Ink* offers us a new
way to pay attention to what we see and allows us a way to document on paper what
we see. Our painting becomes our meditation room.

Traditionally, a meditation room is a clear space, a living painting containing some
talisman of the creative spirit for the eye and heart to contemplate. There is usually
an altar or a small enclosure (*tokonoma* in Japan) containing a simple painting on a
hanging scroll (*kakemono*), and a single flower or sprig or a bowl of fruit appropriate
to the season. Each object has its place. You can re-enter the universe here, feeling
your contour, your own shape in space, able to experience the exhilaration of spareness, of simplicity, of light. There is room enough for you here.

The purpose of *A Meditation in Ink* is to help you create this same feeling, this inner meditation room, as you paint. A cluttered painting is distracting, while a blank
sheet awaits only you to create the life in its space. The insights of your inner eye
translated onto paper give creative expression to your universe.

How to Paint.   Your painting space can be your bedroom, study, workroom, or kitch-
en table. You may paint sitting, standing, or kneeling, alone or with others. What is
important about creating a painting environment is that you feel it is your "safe"
space, a place where you will be free to close your eyes, to dawdle, to experiment, to
paint without being interrupted by the tensions of the universe. It is your meditation
room.

Painting requires some preparation — selecting the time, assembling the materials,
setting the mood. Whether you paint at the same time every day or once a week, you
will establish a routine. Routines make life simpler. They can also lull you to sleep.
As you turn on the water to prepare your tea — be aware. As you spread a protective
layer of newspaper or felt on your painting surface — be aware. As you drink your
tea — be aware. So, too, during the gentle, rhythmical grinding of the ink on the ink
stone. Watching carefully the dark liquid trickling into the well, notice how the water
and ink intermingle. Be aware of the blackest black your ink can produce.

When you close your eyes to mediate, your attention will turn inward. But as you
begin to paint, it will turn outward again. As you look at the blank white paper, keep
your attention on both the inner and outer universe. With the subject before you, or
perhaps brought to mind through your meditation, dip your brush into the ink. Before
you paint, pay attention to your breath, letting your brush circle freely in the air
until you know intuitively where to make the first stroke. Execute it with a single

X

exhalation of breath. As you paint, continue to be aware of your breath, whether you are using firm, rough strokes or delicate, sweeping ones. Pay attention to variations of color and texture in the subject and in the painting. Be aware as you make some areas dark and strong in the foreground, others light and misty in the background. And then when you stop a moment to consider — be aware — and put down your brush. A painting is best left unfinished rather than overdone. Setting your painting aside, be aware of the feelings or thoughts you are having about your work. As you relax with a fresh cup of tea, be aware of ending one painting and beginning another. And as you take a fresh sheet of paper and dip your brush into the well of ink once again — be aware!

How to Use This Book. While *A Meditation in Ink* is about the "inner" life of sumi-e, ultimately it is about the "inner" life of each of us. This book began with two purposes, as a documentation of my own painting experience and as an alternative to the usual "how-to" method of teaching found in books. The danger was that it might become on the one hand a mystical treatise and on the other a theoretical flight. However, my intention has been at every step to make sumi-e and the methodology of my meditations readily accessible and understandable. As such, it is actually a workbook designed to take you through the process of sumi-e painting as *A Meditation in Ink.*

This book may be read in several ways. You may read it through from the beginning to the end in one sitting before actually beginning to paint. Or you may turn first to the last two chapters to find out the "basics" before experiencing one of the meditations. Or you may want to dally, reading and tasting whatever appeals to you. Perhaps in reading over the Table of Contents you are attracted to a specific exercise in Chapter Four. Go ahead and do it. Perhaps you have been painting sumi-e (or another medium) for many years, but are interested in trying the new approach suggested by the Basic Meditations of Chapter Three. Or you may be a watercolorist searching for a Japanese inscription to add to a flower painting. You will find this in the appendices. There, too, you can, if you wish, find a school to study sumi-e, or a place to buy your materials. This book is intended as a resource tool for beginners and more advanced students as well. As such, it will serve its purpose, however you choose to use it.

A Meditation in Ink offers to guide you to becoming your own teacher and your own student. The process explored in this book allows sumi-e to be lit from the inside, providing you with immediate accessibility and swiftness of application, granting the capacity for humor, mistakes, and mind-stretching, and generating unending variety. This book is a "round" that requires your own sound to complete the song. Sumi-e is offered to you to be enjoyed and expanded to the full without the necessity of a teacher or a lengthy apprenticeship. In this time of growing alienation and technological displacement, the meditations described in this book map not only the path of sumi-e, but a way back to the solid ground of our own being.

ACKNOWLEDGMENTS

The process of bringing this book to completion depended upon a living meditation. Like a cup of tea before painting, Sam Julty started me off on this project and provided invaluable support and assistance when my cup ran dry. The fabric of my paper was woven by my teachers, Kwok Kay Choey, Koho Yamamoto, Siuling Wong, and Motoi Oi. Good quality ink was provided by Jess Kalish and Mark Spilkowitz, who helped with the photography, Sharon Nakazato, who, in addition to assisting with the photography, also provided "Calligraphy Practice" and the research and calligraphy for the list of Japanese phrases in the Appendix, and Joan Rosinsky, whose typing prevented this book from being an ink blot. My editors and their colleagues provided a *suzuri* which ground fine and well. Like the many strands of a good brush, my students have helped me focus my energy into a sure point which can spread water and ink even and smooth on the paper. And the water supporting all has been Mara Sandler, whose clearness and nourishment provided continual support, inspiration, and renewal to both my brushes and myself.

ABOUT THE AUTHOR

"Visual forms have always had a powerful impact on me," Paul Siudzinski recollects. "Besides the natural environment, museums such as the Albright-Knox in Buffalo educated me in the basic elements of line, form and color."

After completing his formal education at the State University of New York at Buffalo, and graduate studies at the University of New Hampshire and the University of Wisconsin, Siudzinski traveled extensively in the Far East. He settled in Kyoto, Japan, where he lived and worked for two years. It was here that he first came in contact with sumi-e. "I saw someone pick up a sumi brush and paint bamboo in slow motion. It was magic. In that moment, my direction became clear."

After returning to the United States, Siudzinski embarked on a career as a painter and writer. He established a Meditation in Ink in New York City, a school for the study of sumi-e and other arts. Siudzinski exhibits and sells his work in galleries around New York. He makes his home in Northport, New York.

Japanese Brush Painting Techniques

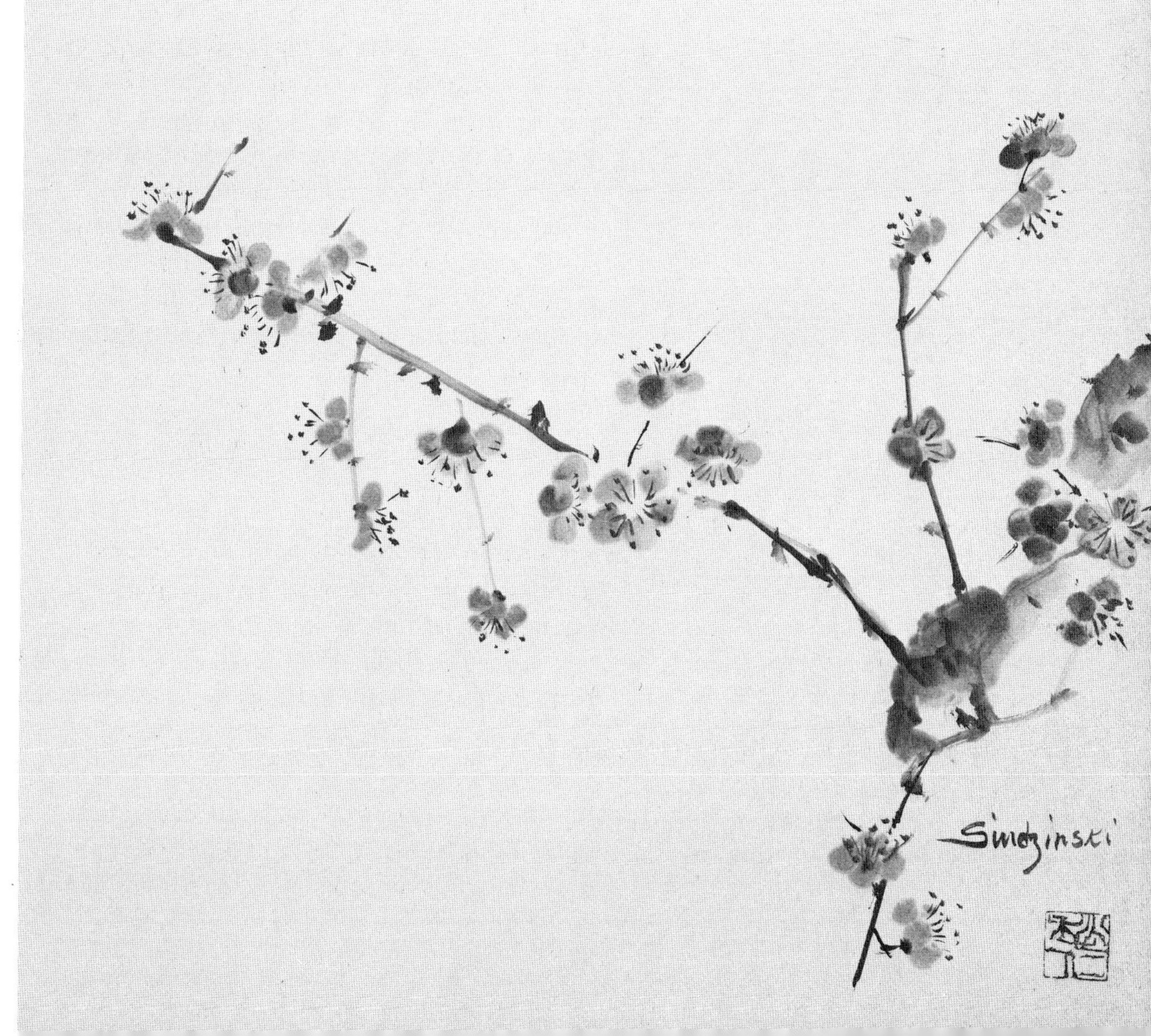

Chapter 1

INTRODUCTION

"I don't know anything about painting," is often the first thing a student tells me upon entering the studio. Everyone wants to paint well, but it is difficult to paint if you are tense, if you think people are judging your work, and, most of all, if you are comparing yourself to others, trying to paint a painting as it is "supposed" to look.

One student came to me so tense about what she thought she didn't know that had she been swimming she would have drowned in a knot. "I can't even paint a straight line," she told me. A cup of tea and our group meditation seemed to relax her, but she still appeared uneasy. I began to work with her individually, as I do with everyone in the class. I asked her to breathe into her body and then encouraged her to notice her physical sensations, to note her feelings and attitudes as she painted. As she followed my instructions, the choked, spastic lines that she had been painting began to disappear, and long, sure lines began to flow onto her paper. I left her clearly involved and went on to the next student. Later, when I looked over at her, she was happily and intently teaching herself how to paint bamboo.

It wasn't until the next class that she confided to me, "I've never been able to paint. Last week I overcame a lifelong block I had about doing things with my hands. I was so proud of myself, I hung my pictures on the wall!"

The men and women who take my classes come from many walks of life — businessmen and -women, housewives, teachers, students, hairstylists, advertising executives, dancers, painters, social workers, therapists. They range in age from teens to septuaganarians, and they bring divergent points of view and life experiences. They have their spe-

cial needs. And they make their individual discoveries.

One student who had lost an arm was able to
work on reteaching himself to paint with his
other arm. An advertising executive who had
never tried anything like painting found himself
creating art for the first time in his life. A
father and his daughter found a mutual interest.
A dancer discovered that her brush moved across
the paper the way her body moved through space
while dancing. And a teacher gained new insights into how students learn.

There is a unity behind all this disparate hu-
manity, these people who seem so different and
heterogeneous. They come to my classes feeling
uncertain; yet they are expectant. They come
together partly out of curiosity about who they
might be. They come together, too, out of dis-
content with the way they have been taught, and
with the limitations that have been imposed on
them by teachers who told them they could not
paint. Mostly they come together because of a
sneaking suspicion that underneath the fears and
doubts, there are lines of beauty, waiting to
come out.

Much of what I say can be applied to other
disciplines — acting, sports, writing — but I talk
primarily about painting. You will notice, however, that I do not stress technique alone. Techniques do not make people into painters. My
students, especially those who felt they could
not paint, have taught me that we are all painters. It is a matter of tuning into the inner landscape, and allowing that sense to move the brush.
When we listen well to ourselves, our best paintings can happen. This book is about that process.

Ichimon-ji. The sprig and the
ceramic jug each have a different
texture and a different inner life.
You must experience this difference before you can paint it.

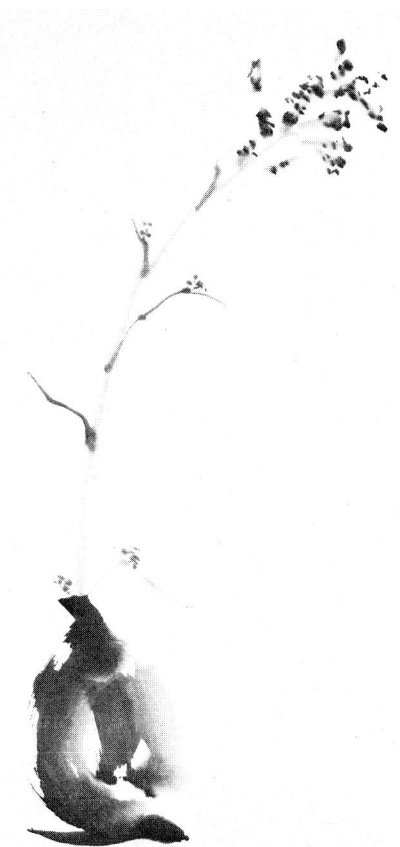

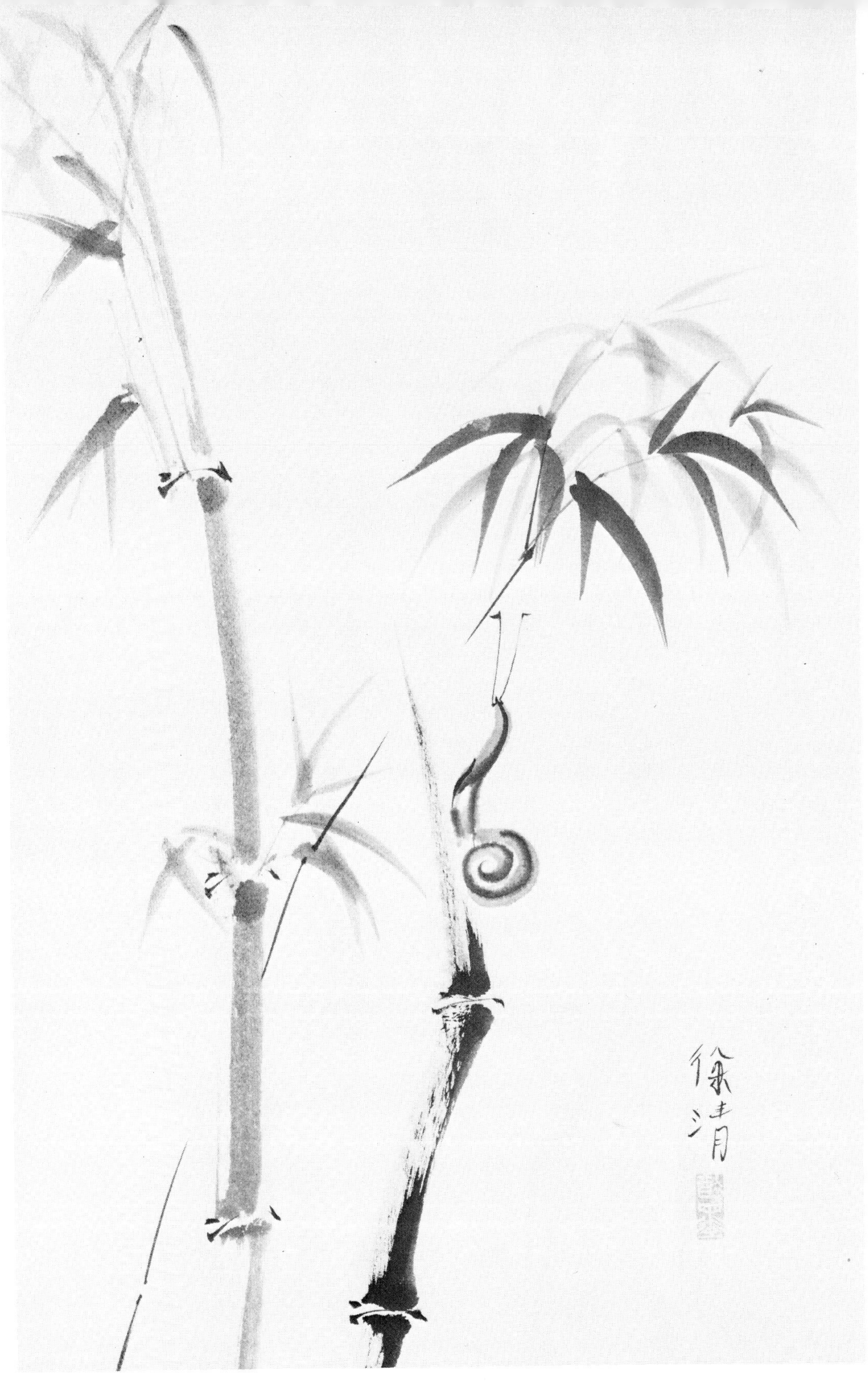

The Enlightened Snail.

Chapter 2

BEGINNER'S MIND

*Nan-in, a Japanese master during the Meiji era, received a visiting scholar who came to inquire about Zen. Nan-in served tea. He poured his visitor's cup full, and then kept on pouring. The scholar watched the overflow until he could no longer restrain himself. "It is overfull. No more will go in!" "Like this cup," Nan-in said, "you are full of your own opinions and speculations. How can I show you Zen unless you first empty your cup?"**

Has your mind sometimes been like the teacup — overflowing? If you have tried to make your mind empty, you know how difficult it is to do what the Zen master instructs. As soon as you close your eyes, you are beseiged by an

---

*Adapted from *Zen Flesh, Zen Bones: A Collection of Zen and Pre-Zen Writings*, compiled by Paul Reps (Tokyo, Tuttle, 1957), p. 19.

How to Laugh. Not all paintings need a living source. Daikoku, one of the seven lucky gods of Japan, symbolizes luck and happiness. Originally a Chinese monk who carried around in his bag an assortment of goodies for children, he was transformed into a Japanese god who now carries the riches of the world.

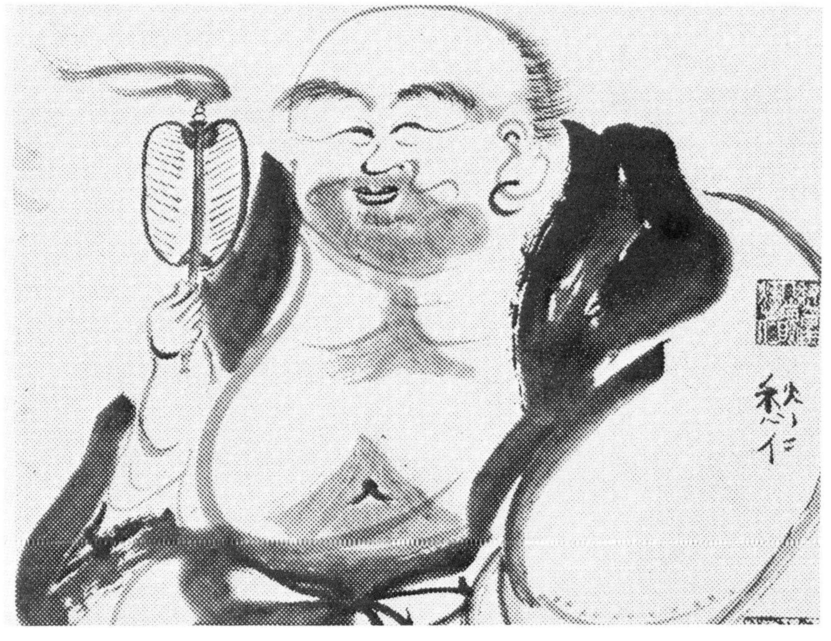

overfull mind. How are you to empty out this
chattering cup? At best, you are told, "Let your
mind empty itself."

Zen painters approach painting in the spirit
of meditation. They paint like beginners, straight-
forwardly, simply, innocently. They do not try
to paint pictures that are beautiful or skillful
or try to make the subject look the way it is
"supposed to." Because they "pay attention,"
as if seeing something for the first time, their
paintings are full of vitality. To pay attention
like this is to capture the inner spirit of the subject. To follow the way of the brush is to paint
with the beginner's mind.

A Painter Is a Dancer with a Brush

We all know the difference between self-conscious-
ly watching ourselves dance and being swept up by
the music. When we simply allow our body to
move, the mind empties. Knowing we are free and
one with the music, we experience an exhilarating
feeling of release. The energy that comes from being directly connected to our inner self is so powerful that even those who do not consider themselves dancers will, at such moments, want to
"dance all night."

Painting, like dancing and many other everyday
activities — bike riding, roller-skating, cooking,
writing, even typing — can be viewed as a form of
meditation. There comes a moment when you are
totally absorbed in being what you do. You and
your activity have become one.

Yet there is a part of you that stands aside —
a still part — and watches the process without in-
terfering. This observer, this inner eye, knows
what you are about in a very clear-sighted way.
The way of the brush is to pay attention with the
inner eye.

What keeps us from paying attention? We have
already noted the chattering in our heads. There

Full or Empty.

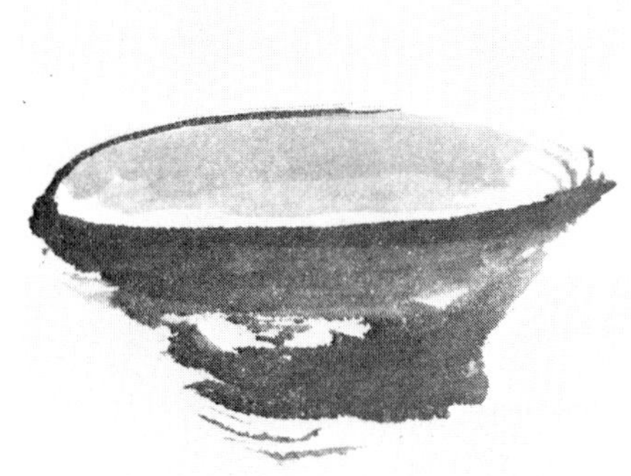

6

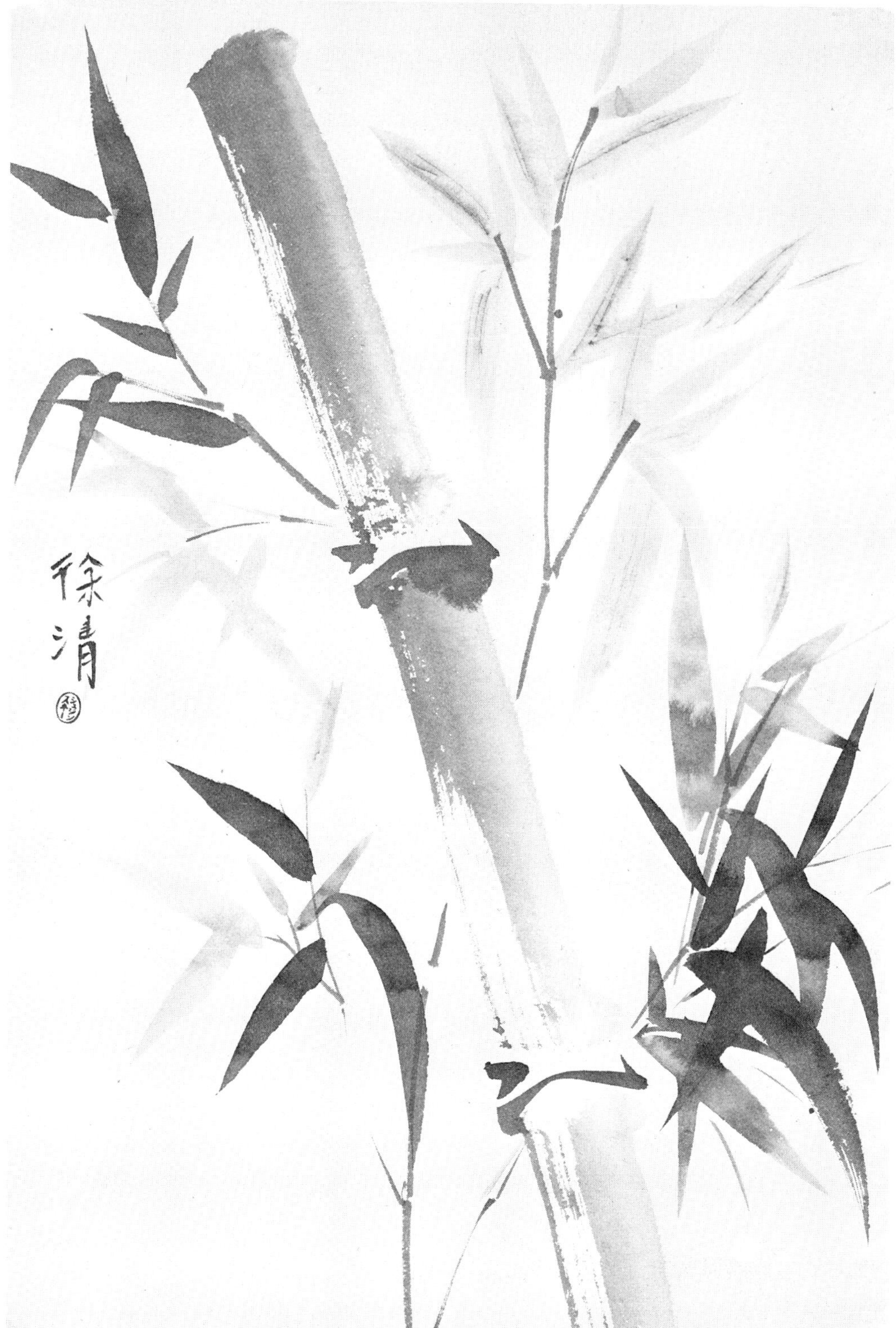

Leaf Blanket. A single bole of bamboo swaddled in leaves gives an effect of lushness. The "dry brush" of the bamboo creates the mood of a rainy day. This is heightened by the shadowy leaves at lower right and the streaky quality of those at upper right.

is yet another element that overcomes us — habit — a boring fellow. He is always sleeping. For example, listening to a popular song, we may not actually "hear" it, because we know it so well. The same is true of the things we look at every day without seeing, the talks we have without communicating, the motions we make without touching. Habit.

Paradox 1: Look around you at this moment and see what you are not paying attention to.

Paradox 2: Look at something without knowing its name.

Paying attention means to "see" something and not know what it is. When we paint a leaf, each moment of seeing is new. This newness is what moves our brush. The leaf simply moves through us onto the paper, like a dancer whose energy moves the body gracefully through space. A painter is like a dancer with a brush.

A Meditation in Ink

The painting on page 9 captures my experience of paying attention. It is a meditation in ink, a finger painting that I completed in two or three minutes. There is no brushwork to speak of because I used my fingers as a brush. It is important in this kind of painting to know what the subject is before picking up the brush. Therefore, I began by first clearing my mind with a series of centering and relaxation exercises. When I started to paint, I knew what I wanted to say but was uncertain what form the bird would take. My fingers knew; I stood aside and watched as the bird painted itself. After that I watched my sense of the scene and my feelings and other "seeings" paint a branch that was right for the bird to rest on; then another rough branch at the bottom, empty and waiting. My main sense throughout the painting was of watching an uninterrupted flow of ink onto the paper. The white space was a universe ready to be startled into breathing

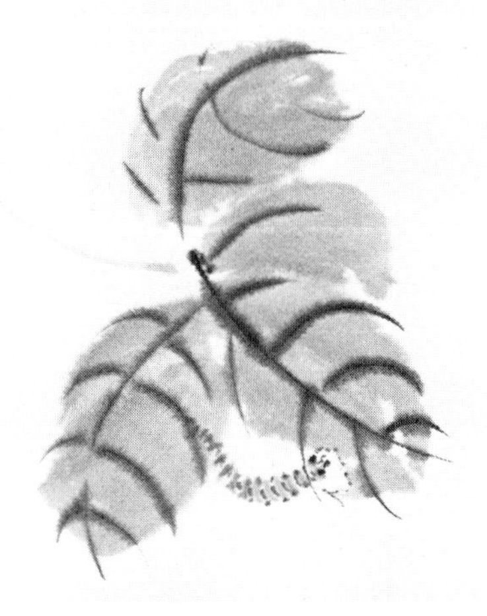

Free-Floating. These leaves were painted with two bilateral strokes, which quickly bled together. The darker veins were added before the leaf dried.

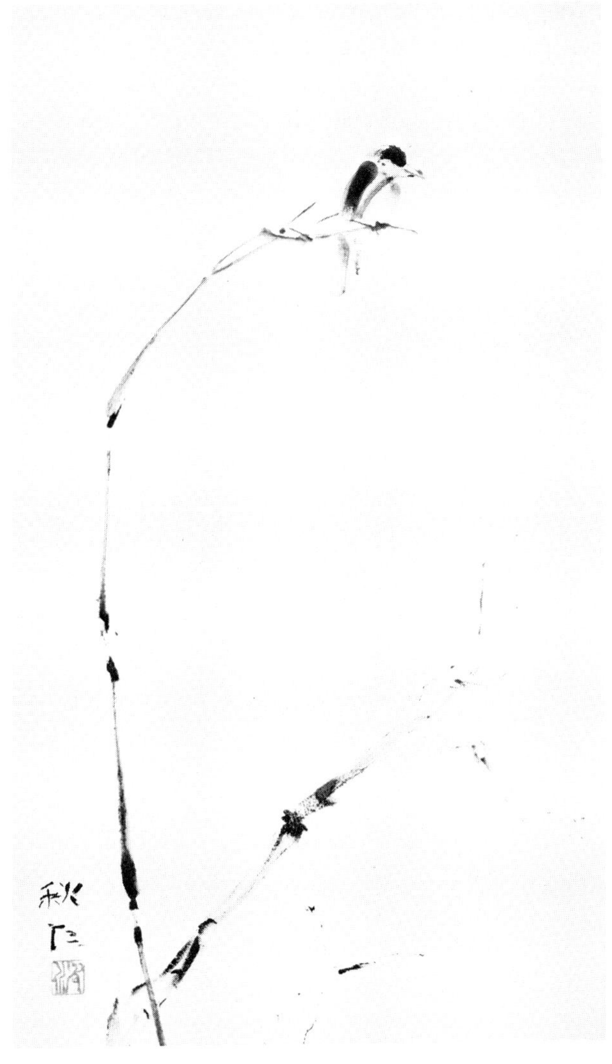

Paying Attention.

forms. My fingers cooperated. It was a cohesive
and uninterrupted experience. Stylistically, the
painting is rough and sketchy; but the inner experience was as clear as the space that supports
the bird swaying on the branch.

This painting is alive because it is actually two
paintings, an outer painting, clearly seen as a bird,
a branch, and so on, and an inner painting, a
sort of spirit which enlivens the brush strokes,
liberated through meditation. Sumi-e has its
source in the inner painting, the experience of
paying attention and seeing; the outer painting is
the record of the inner experience.

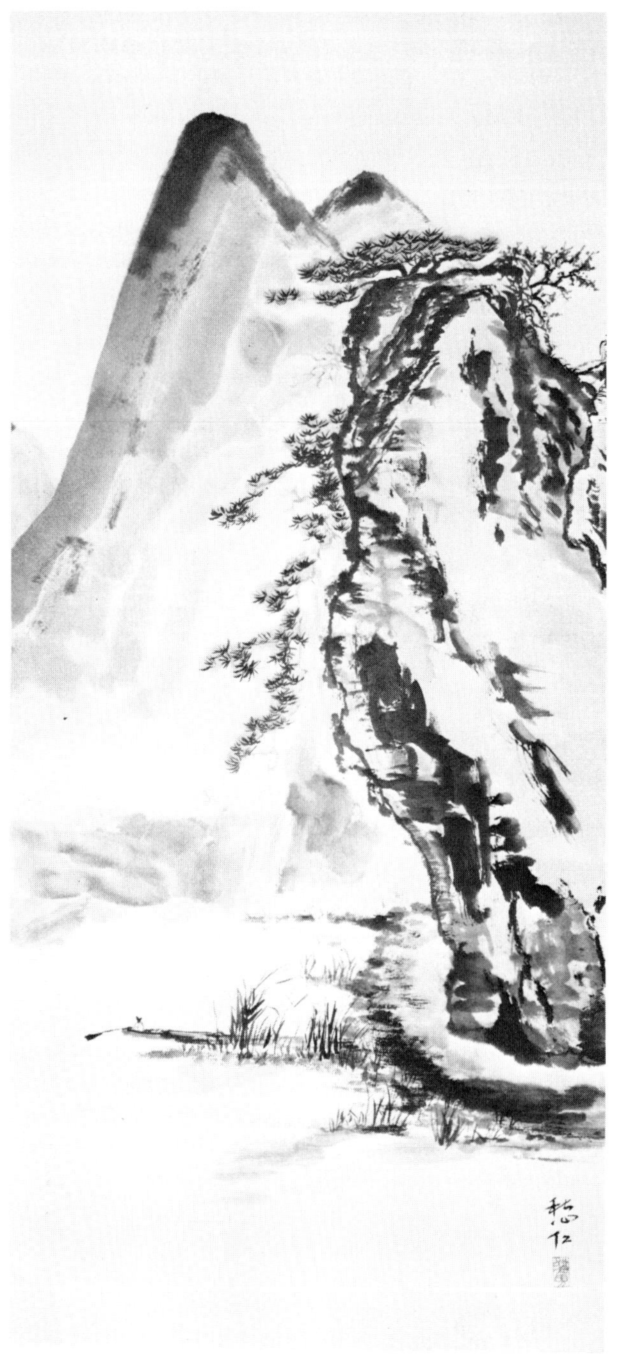

Meditations through the Senses

The Sound of the Mountain, a novel by Yasunari
Kawabata, is about family life as seen by an old

10

man in rapidly changing Japan. Uncertain of himself and his values, he imagines occasionally he can hear the mountain behind his house moving. This link with nature is at once terrifying and reassuring, for the sound of the mountain is a symbol of the crushing weight of tradition, of the forces of change, of death. Most important, however, is that the old man hears the sound; this is a connection to reality, to his own nature.

In painting it is essential to capturè the spirit of the subject. Our senses are one way we have of knowing and becoming familiar with what we paint, of feeling what its "life" is like. One sense may predominate, the sight or smell of a flower, the sound or motion of a stormy bamboo grove, the taste of an orange or a peach. But everything is sensuous; everything has taste, smell, touch, sound, and vision. Even a rock has a sound and a taste.

Feelings, thoughts, and moods can also help us understand a subject. The sound of a bamboo flute playing in the background can be translated with awareness into a serene bamboo grove. Thoughts can be utilized to discover new subjects for painting. It is possible to use the emotions to paint some very energized and exciting lines, even whole paintings. There is an old Japanese maxim, "When angry, paint bamboo; when happy, paint the iris." Awareness of what we are doing or feeling can help us connect the inner painting to the outer painting.

A Meditation in Ink is a constant process of paying attention to what we are doing. Paying attention will help us to remember ourselves, will reconnect our inner painting to the outer painting, and will enable us to create the paintings we want, to "see" what we are painting.

The Inner Painting

The subject matter, materials, and techniques of the inner painting are as various and complicated

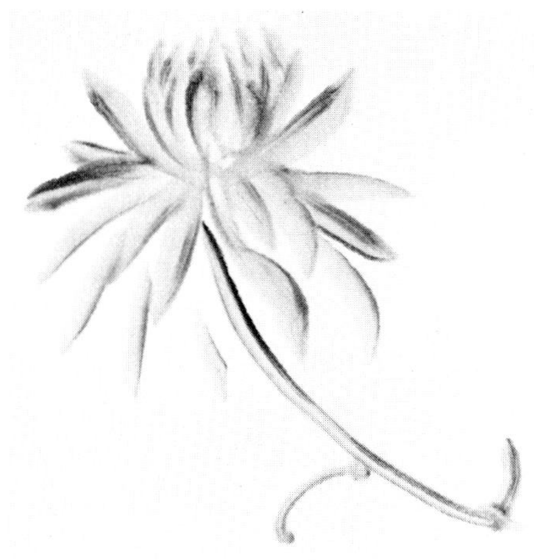

Soft Bouquet. The coloring of this long-petaled chrysanthemum is brought out by contrasting darker outlines, which were added before the grey ink of the petals dried, creating a soft, blurred effect. The two-colored stem was created by putting dark ink on one side of the brush only.

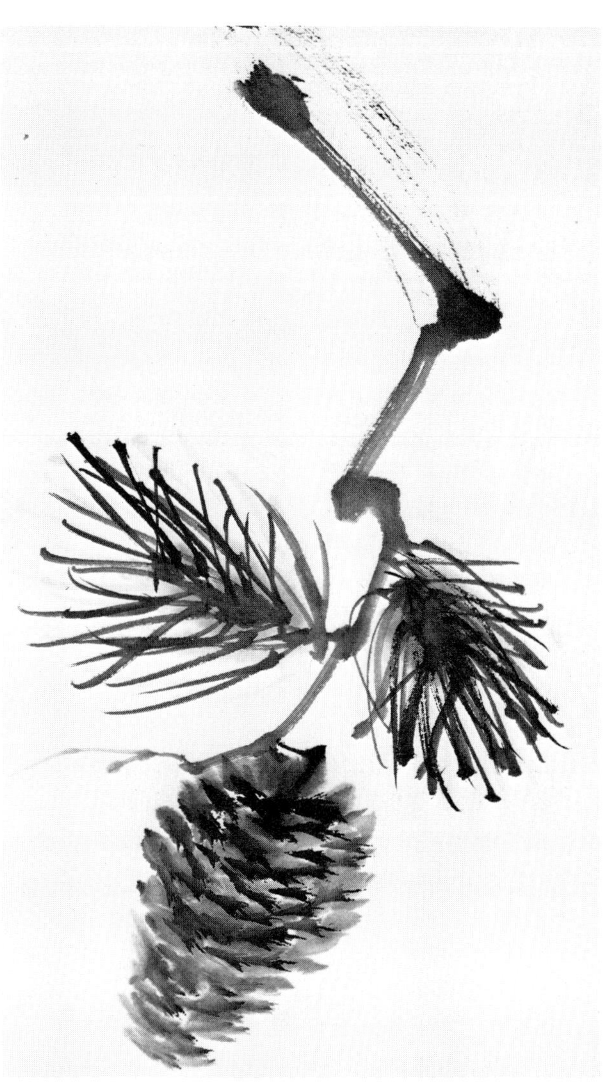

Falling Cone.

as those of the outer painting. If you can imagine
what it is like to paint a picture of a bamboo
grove on a quiet rainy day, you will realize that
the painting demands a certain awareness, feeling,
and participation. To paint bamboo on a rainy day
actually requires that we understand what it is to
live and grow as bamboo and that we feel the mood
and quality of a rainy day in a bamboo grove. Although we are painting in a kitchen, bedroom, or
studio, the rainy bamboo grove will ask that we
ignore the sound of rock 'n' roll music, the smell of

brewing coffee, the pangs of hunger, and the feel of
the mosquito alighting to bite our ankle. Our rainy
bamboo grove will appear peaceful and lovely if
we can be in touch with feelings of solitude and
muted beauty.

The elements that make up the inner painting
are (1) the demands of the subject; (2) our internal
emotional, mental, and intuitive life; and (3) our
sensuous awareness of the world around us. All
are important. All contribute to the strength and
beauty of a realized painting. The meditations described in the next two chapters will provide you
with the tools you need to explore these elements.

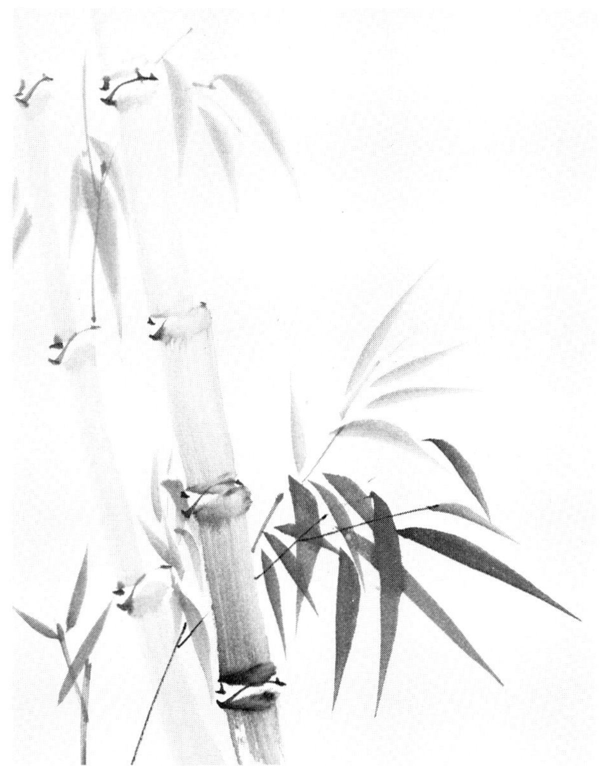

Rainy Day. Here all the bamboo
leaves are of different sizes, no two
in exactly the same plane or pointed
in the same direction. The main interest of the painting is the contrast
between the misty and subdued
bamboo on the left and the energet-
ic, searching leaves on the right.

Chapter 3

THE BASIC MEDITATIONS

I always begin my painting classes with a meditation to help unfold and guide the process of the inner painting. Students report they find it an opening, enlivening experience. They are able to leave behind the tensions of the day, and begin to focus on themselves and what they are feeling and experiencing at the moment. This quiet meditation also helps them prepare for the more active meditation of the sumi-e itself. The meditations are so powerful that my students often say they come to class for the meditation, not the painting!

I have discovered that if I do not meditate, it takes an hour or two before my paintings start to develop. If I meditate before painting, however, my paintings take on an immediate vitality. You may not be aware of this difference in your early painting sessions. But if you meditate with an activity you are already skilled at, you will notice the difference immediately. This same qualitative difference will become apparent to you with your painting as you acquire more experience.

A painting session usually begins with a cup of tea, either herbal tea or Japanese tea. The tea is a gift to yourself. It also signifies a clearing away of the last "meal" and the beginning of a new "meal." Warmed by the pleasure and relaxation of a leisurely cup of tea, you will find it a pleasure to close your eyes and begin your meditation.

Meditation is a skill that you can learn easily. These meditations are structured specifically for painting. If you have had previous experience at meditation, it is all to the better, as you will be making new discoveries and connections.

The first meditation is designed to teach you how to use your breath to explore, relax, and en-

Multiplying Onions. Common fruits and vegetables are so familiar to us, we can easily overlook them when searching for a subject to paint. Capturing their essence in ink is like looking up old friends. Two onions were rearranged several times for this painting.

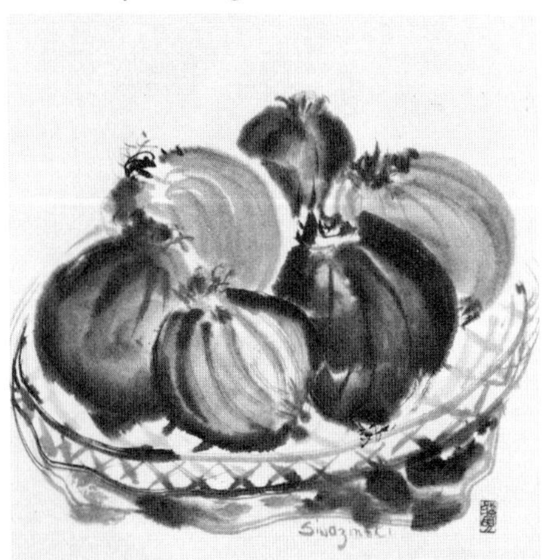

liven your body. Your paintings will flow from
within, and it is your breath that will give life and
expression to your paintings.

The second meditation turns outward to teach
you how to look at the objects you will paint.
While you will be focusing on an external object,
notice that you will be using the knowledge gained
about yourself in the first meditation.

These first two meditations, "Centering" and
"Seeing," are designed to be done again and again.
It is recommended that you begin each painting
session with the first meditation, and if you are
painting from a live model, the second as well.
If you develop your meditative ability early, you
will soon find it becoming almost second nature;
you will begin to meditate even as you set out
your materials.

The other meditations in this chapter will help
you explore and develop aspects of the relationship between the inner and the outer paintings.
They are all begun before you pick up your brush,
but some, like the music meditations, can easily
extend into your painting time as well.

Basic Meditation 1:
    Centering through the Breath

This basic meditation should begin each painting
session. It is done with the eyes closed. It may
be done sitting in a chair, or, if you practice yoga,
in any of the familiar sitting positions. When you
are comfortable, yet alert, close your eyes and
focus on your breathing. There is no need to try
to change your breathing, but only to be aware
of the rhythm. Through the breath, you will re-

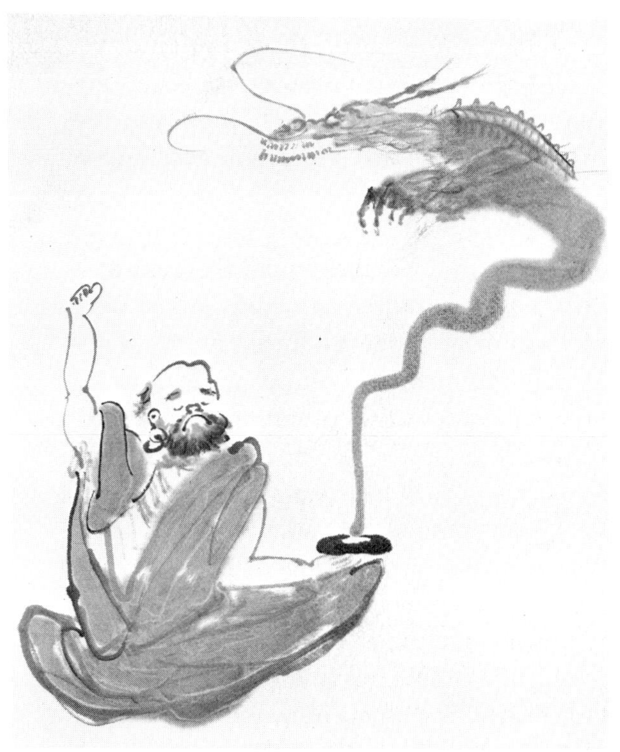

lease tensions and relax your body. Beginning
with your feet, then, feel the floor, the bottoms
of your feet, and your toes. Moving up the legs,
be aware of your ankles, calves, knees, thighs.
For each point, take one breath of time to feel
it, then move on to the next place. Now be
aware of your buttocks and the surface supporting you. Move up to your stomach and chest, your
lower, middle, and upper back. Feel your entire
spine, and send a deep breath through it, as if it
were a hollow reed; feel it as your moving center,
the brush that moves your body. Now proceed to
your shoulders, upper arms, elbows, forearms,
wrists, hands, and fingers. Finally, your neck, chin,
mouth, nose, eyes, forehead, face, the back of your
head, the top of your head, your entire head. Experience your head as a luminous globe of light.

As you breathe, remember to send the breath
to each of the stopping points as you move through
your body. You will soon be able to identify the
tension spots, and send relaxing breaths to these
areas.

Now notice all five of your senses. You will
feel the floor and your chair, the sensation of your
clothes, the warmth or coolness of the air. If you
had tea before beginning the meditation, you may
still taste it in your mouth. You will be able to
hear the sound of traffic, of dinner being prepared,
of the radio playing, of your own breathing.
Breath is your focus throughout all these sensations, centering your mind, allowing you to view
everything as if from a distance, but always returning you to yourself.

You will also have thoughts and memories,
feelings and emotions, ideas and opinions, of people you have seen, of tasks undone, and more,
drifting through your mind. All this you can let
be, without trying to banish any of it. Breath is
the thread through the continuing fluctuations of
mood, feelings, and experiences in your meditation. Focusing on the breath is the way of letting
go, of experiencing the inside, of getting grounded
in your center.

When you are ready to end the meditation, re-

Study in Yellow and Green. This
painting of bamboo, based on an
old study, is a very stylized portrayal in only two colors. It is clear
that leaves and stems are of different colors and qualities.

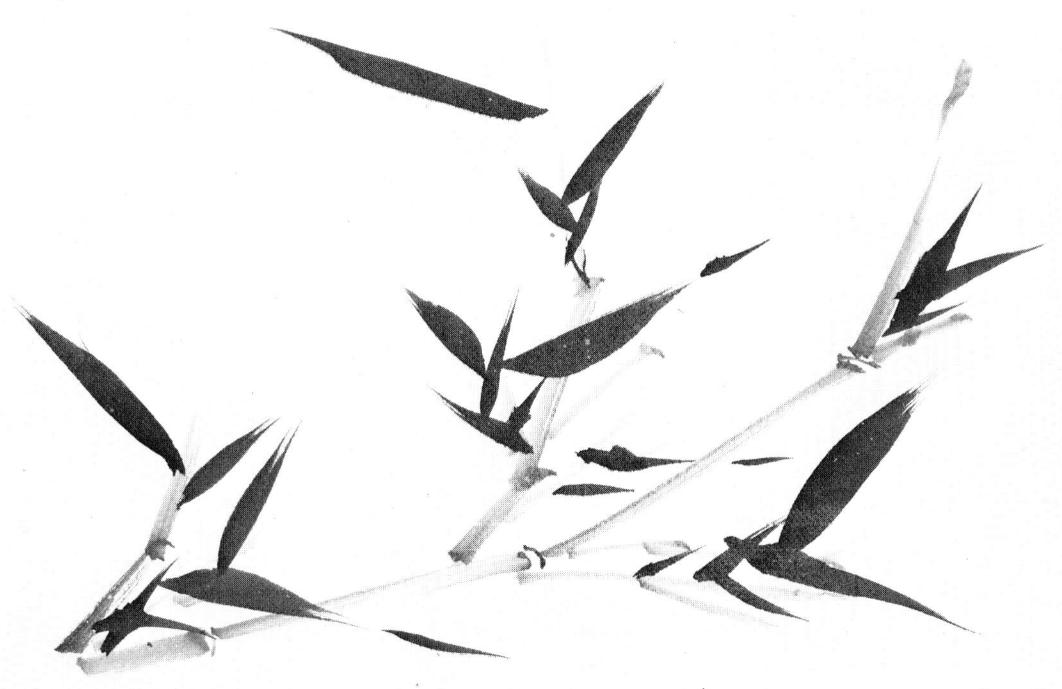

collect the room you are in, the objects around you, their shapes and colors, and then slowly open your eyes, feeling relaxed and refreshed. When you are ready, you may begin to paint.

Basic Meditation 2:
Seeing

Everything you paint has its own "inner meditation," its own way of being. Your painting will reflect your knowledge of the inner life of your subject, how you see into the mystery of its being. To see requires vision in all of the senses, to feel with the eyes and even, as Wordsworth said, to hear "a soft eye-music of slow-waving boughs ..."

You will need a leaf, twig, or flower for this meditation. When you look for something to paint, you will find that certain objects seem to choose you! It is best to begin with something

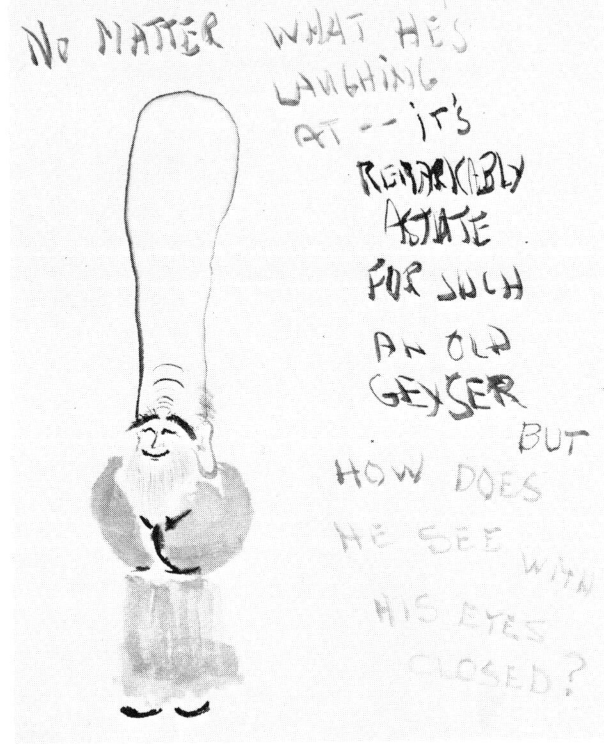

How Does He See? Fukurokuju, another of the lucky gods, symbolizes long life and the wisdom of age. This kind of genre painting, combining words and images, the Japanese call *Haiga*. The face and head were painted first; the body was completed in only a few strokes.

small. However, of the several things you are attracted to, a leaf or a flower is probably best. Now sit down with it and find out what makes it unique. Of all others of its kind, what is special about this flower, this leaf?

To get to know your subject, first set it down in front of you and simply look at it. Everything you paint has a center; a rose unfolds from its center, as does a leaf, a tree, and every living creature. You have a center, too. Just as in meditation you pay attention to yourself to find your own center, look carefully at your leaf or sprig and find its center to paint it. The parts of a sprig, for example, will project in four directions; those closer to you will appear larger, those farther away smaller. Notice that the tops of leaves will be darker than the undersides; the branches will be of a different texture from the leaves. Also notice the veins and how they glide into the leaf.

Pick up the sprig and rotate it so you can see all sides. Notice the changing perspectives, the shadows, the light. How do the different groups of leaves or the different parts of one leaf relate to each other?

Now close your eyes and feel the surface of the leaf without looking. Rub it against your cheek, your eyelids; smell it, taste it. Feel its weight in your hands, its delicate arrangement. And listen to it, too. Let it tell you what other lives have touched it, what seasons it has held, what the journey up from its dark roots was like. Leaves respond to voices, so you might try talking to your leaf and sharing with it some of your own thoughts.

When you open your eyes, be aware that you may be looking at your leaf without "knowing" what it is, simply "seeing" it without its name. This is how you will paint it. Clearly and precisely, you will record its texture and color, its solidity or lightness, its projections into space, which part is forward, which only partly seen.

Knowing your leaf does not mean you will

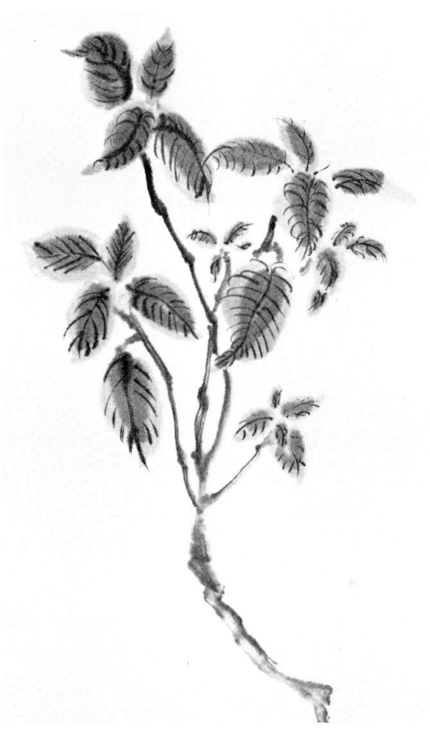

Growth. Painting live subjects is the most exciting and demanding way to paint. When you paint, you must notice the turn of each leaf, the depth of each leaf cluster, the relative sizes of leaves, the strength of the stems.

paint an exact copy, realistic to the last detail. This is not the style of sumi-e, nor the purpose of this meditation. You will have captured the spirit of the leaf, however; knowing what makes this leaf different from all other leaves will enable your inner painting to give life to the outer painting.

Having completed one or both of these basic meditations, you will find several directions open to you. You may wish to paint, staying aware of the many aspects of the inner painting as you go along. You may want to explore another subject or mood more deeply using another of the meditations you will find in this book. You may want to devise your own. Throughout, it is essential that you remain aware of the inner focus and the rhythmical cycle of your breathing, because this is your bridge from the timelessness of your inner being to the outer world and the present. It will focus you on what is solid, real, and important in both the inner and the outer painting.

A Pond in Spring. Painting from nature can be relaxing or exciting, depending on your mood. Here the polywogs give life to the foreground, while the background is peaceful and quiet.

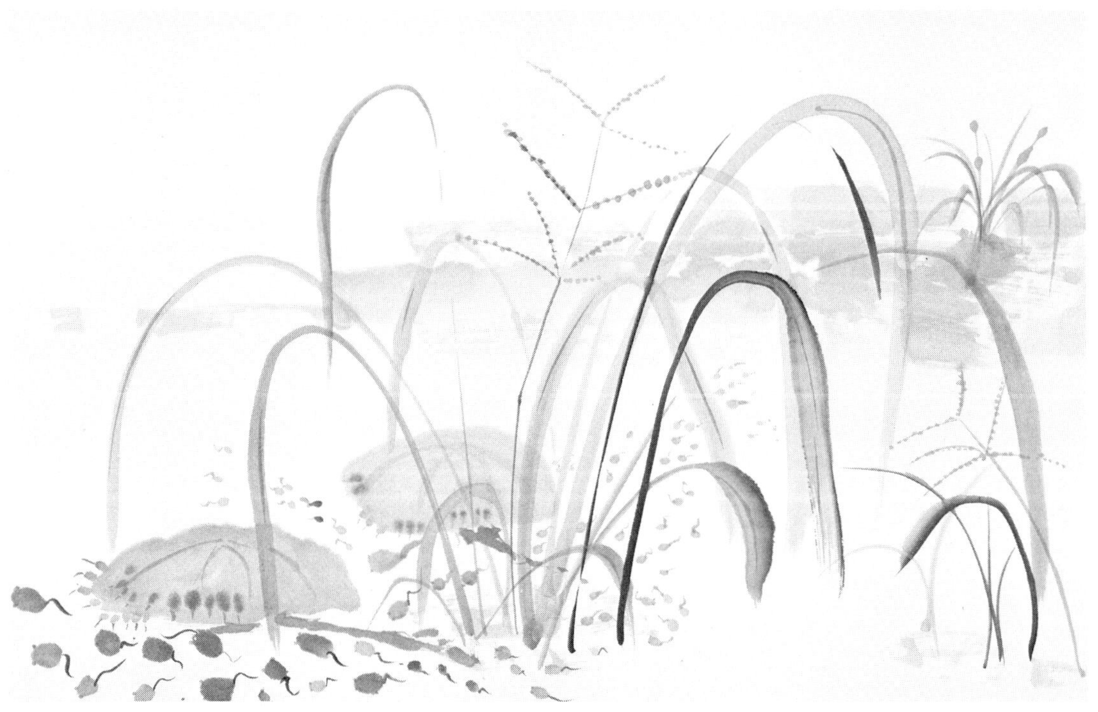

Further Meditations

"Meditations to Music" and "Fantasy Journeys,"
like the basic meditations, are wellsprings to be
drawn upon again and again, each time offering
renewing nourishment for your painting process.
Through my own painting experience, I developed
these exercises, and have used them in my classes.
Process-oriented rather than product-oriented,
they allow you to grow and gain insight into how
you see the world and yourself. They are depend-
ent upon your participation and attention; and
they will continue to be a way to see things so
long as you keep listening to yourself. As you
grow, your natural wisdom and creativity will in-
creasingly make themselves felt in your paintings.

    These exercises are done inwardly after first cen-
tering yourself and focusing on your breathing.
There are no strict rules, however, and you may
have your own methods of inducing relaxation.
You will quickly discover which exercises are particularly useful because they give you the informa-
tion and insights you need to evolve with your
painting. As you continue to paint, you will create your own meditations as you need them to pay
attention to the places that are most important for
your own seeing.

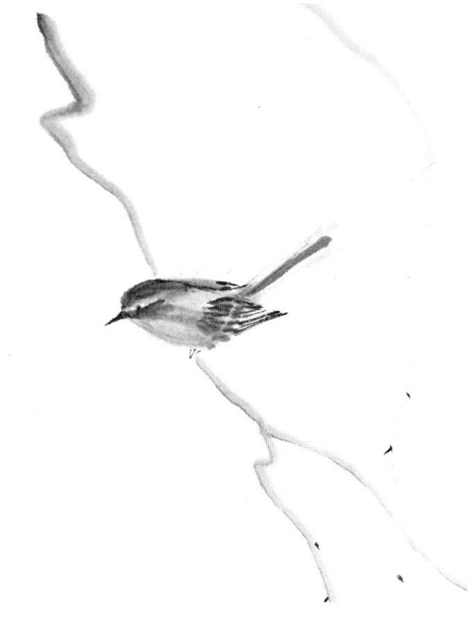

Temporary Rest. A very small subject can give the impression of much
energy and potential movement.
The music of a contemporary Japanese song gave the bird its rhythm.

Meditations to Music

*If you see deep enough, you see
musically; The heart of nature
being everywhere musical, if you
can only reach it. — Carlyle.*

Music has always been the truest voice of our hu-
manity, our stake in hope, inspiration, and renewal. Like nature itself, it is readily available, and
offers unending paths to our inner voice, and outward expression of that voice. How can we draw

from its springs of vitality nourishment for our own creative spirit?

When we begin a meditation to music, our listening patterns should always first include the basic relaxation technique, using breath as the focus. When the mind is emptied, it is able to expand and allow natural harmonies and rhythms to enter and reveal new insights, meanings, and seeings. With selected imagery as the guide, a waking dream is able to unfold in the mind.

Meditations using music along with guided imagery or visualizations can easily be a source of inspiration and creativity. You may use some of the following imagery for meditations — a color, memories, a favorite place, a meadow, a brook, a trip up a mountain, a space voyage, the ocean, traveling on a raft, visiting a friend — or you may want to discover your own.

Suggested Music for Meditations

Serene and relaxing music is the best, of course. You may have your own favorites. Or you may try something new.

- Bach: Especially compositions for woodwinds and strings.
- Debussy: *La Mer, Etudes, Prelude to the Afternoon of a Faun.*
- Mozart: Concerto for Flute and Harp, among many possibilities.
- Smetena: *The Muldau.*
- Stravinsky: *The Firebird.*
- Western classical music in general provides a rich treasurehouse of compositions useful for meditation. But there are other sources as well:
- Medieval instrumental music is wonderful for meditations.
- Japanese classical music: Especially music for shakuhachi, koto, or shamisen.
- Music for Zen Meditation, the album by that name.
- Paul Horn: "Paul Horn in the Taj Mahal."
- Cat Stevens: "Hymn to Morning."

And more. Find your own. You will transform
what enters you, and it will emerge in your painting as an expression of your own inner self.

Three kinds of music meditation are offered
here. "Your Energy Fountain" is similar to the
basic meditation for centering; it focuses on ex-
ploring your inner creativity using music instead
of the breath. "Your Tree," like the basic meditation on seeing, focuses outside you, on a specific image or subject, yet asks you to use your inner resources in fantasy. "Your Mood" introduces you to the emotional correlations at your
disposal between the inner and outer landscapes.

Your Energy Fountain

Let the music take you inside your body. You
are looking for the source of your energy. Where
are the deep fountains of your power, strength,
hope, love? Let the music lead you to your deep-
er self, connecting you to your energies and your
true potential. Focus on the vital center of your
personal power. Feel this core — the seat of your
rich resources — alive and connected with the
power of nature. Let the music suggest to you
how to apply your new vitality to your painting.

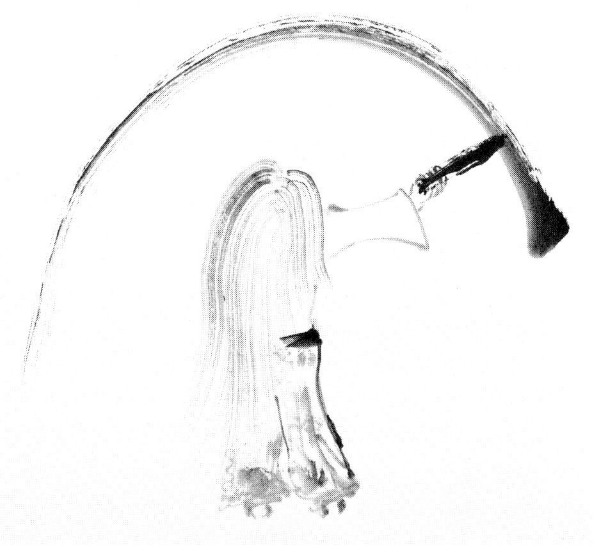

Time or the Rainbow. A mountain,
an entrance, a scythe, all are suggested in what is essentially an enig-
matic and symbolic painting. Personal and impressionistic, the painting came out of my own energy center, but was strongly affected by the
imagery and symbols of death and
rebirth.

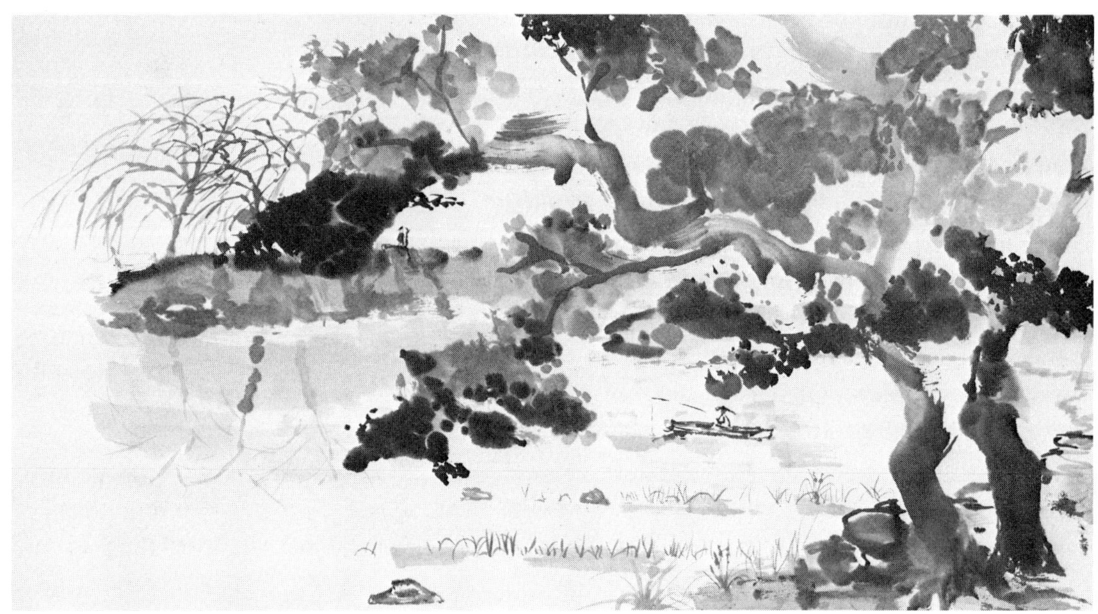

Indian Summer. The lushness of the trees in the foreground is enough to cause us to forget that winter, hovering in the bare branches of the willows across the pond, will soon be with us. This painting was finished in about five minutes.

A Bell Ringing in the Empty Sky. The white space below the simple spray of bamboo is the empty sky into which the swinging movement of the leaves sends its clear sound. Notice the use of color, from very black to light grey to white, white being perhaps the most important color here.

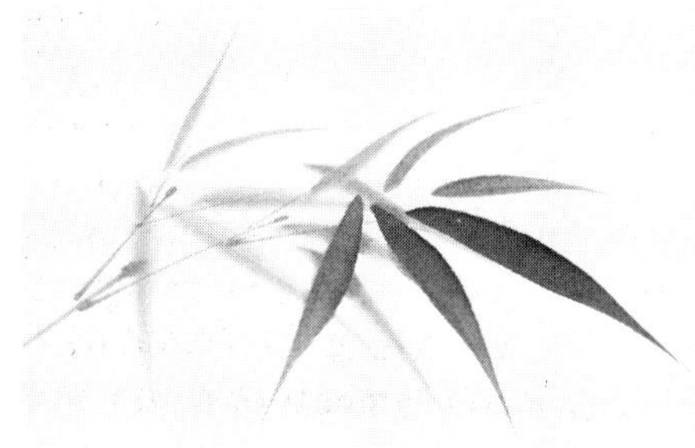

Your Tree

Let the music take you on a search for your tree. Perhaps you will enter a secret garden or find a path in the park. Eventually, you will recognize your tree among many, its shape against the sky, its branches alive with leaves and textures, its colors, its voice in the winds and breezes. Once you find it, communicate with it; in time it will reveal itself to you. Finally, you will take leave of your tree, knowing that you can always return to it. Opening your eyes, allow your seeing of your tree to flow onto the paper. Your painting may hold only one branch, but it will express the essence of your tree.

Your Mood

We all have our favorite places where we have felt moods of loneliness, serenity, or sadness. Listening to music, meditating, visualizing a place that has particular emotional connotations, will help you paint a picture that embodies that feeling or mood.

24

Students entering my studio are often greeted by music, usually a piece called "A Bell Ringing in the Empty Sky." The mood of this musical composition clears away the chatter of the day and creates an immediate meditative space within the studio. A classical solo composition for Japanese *shakuhachi* (bamboo flute), the piece is clear, expansive, and peaceful in spirit. It also communicates loneliness.

A bamboo grove, a landscape, or a pine tree can embody the spiritual quality of "A Bell Ringing in the Empty Sky." Even a tea bowl, if it is painted in the proper spirit. If you meditate on the image of the bell and on the image and feeling of the empty sky, you will discover a special awareness that you can impart to your painting.

This exercise can complement many different moods, images, or settings. If you are in a lonely mood, try finding a musical and pictorial ana-

Feline Fun. Combining elements of cat and tiger, this painting allows a special dimension of each animal to show. The eyes are tigerish, the mouth is kittenish; the wide head and relaxed rear end contrast with the hunched neck and advancing paws. This painting was based on traditional Oriental tiger paintings, but used a live cat as a model. Note the combination of careful detail, as on the face and in the hair, and gross portrayal, as in the body and the stripes.

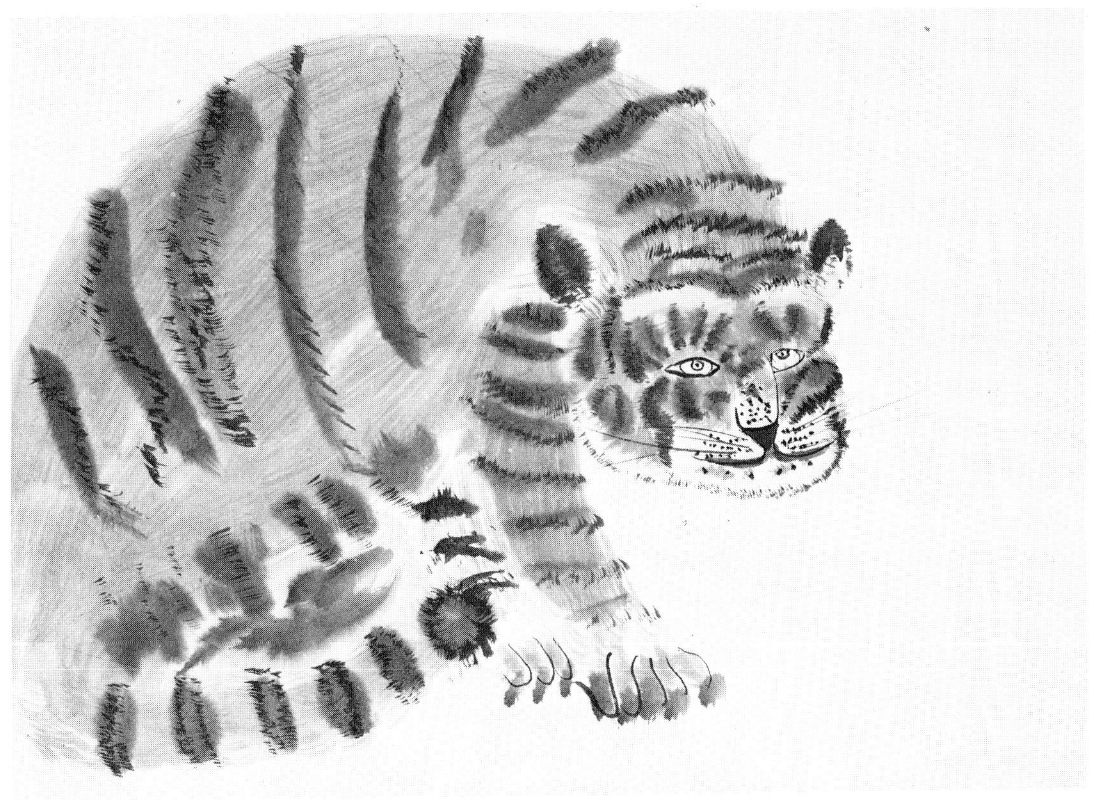

logue for it. You may actually visit a particular place if you want to paint from real life. But listening to music and remembering or imagining such a place may be enough for you to be able to contact and paint your mood meditation.

Fantasy Journeys

Zen paintings portray basic objects, such as teacups and flowers, because it is through common, everyday things and your relationship to them that you will find life's meaning. Learning about the subject you are painting is rather like becoming acquainted and making friends with a person. The range of likes and dislikes in sumi-e, and the possibilities for intimacy and understanding, are as deep as in any relationship. Initial surface explorations soon develop into an empathic kinship and sharing.

Take pottery, for example, the material of the earth. How do you become familiar with something like a Japanese tea bowl? What is there to know about it, after all? Yet a meditation on a tea bowl may start you on an incredible journey — a journey that makes the familiar strange and the strange familiar.

The following meditations are journeys into this realm. The first allows you to become acquainted with a common object, a ceramic tea bowl or cup. The second introduces you to something you have probably never met, Japanese orchids. In painting some traditional sumi-e subjects, like bamboo and orchids, you must rely on photographs, other paintings, and perhaps, in lieu of a visit to Japan, a visit to your local botanical garden. This meditation gives you an additional resource, for it teaches you how to "meet" your subject even though it is thousands of miles away.

Tea Bowl Meditation

Choose a bowl that you really like, or any special piece of pottery, one that you made or that

Tea Ceremony. This bowl, painted in three strokes, could have been painted in two, but at the last I added the bottom line to support the bowl. Notice the almost monochromatic nature of the painting. The black line around the rim was made with a dab of black ink on the tip of an otherwise grey brush. The black tip "flipped" as I reached the left edge, and went down the left side of the bowl instead of continuing along the rim — one of those accidents that commonly produce uncommon results.

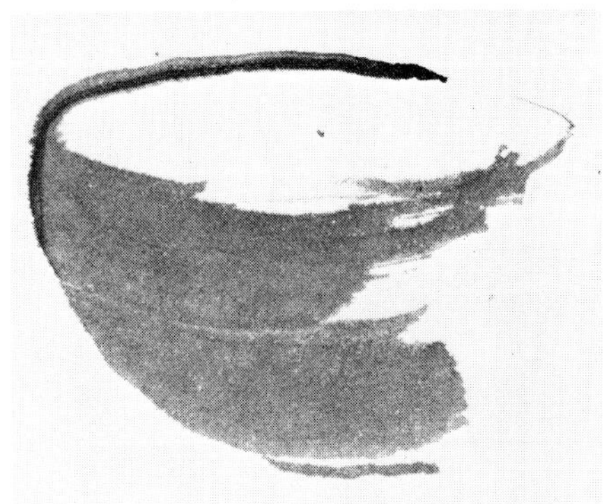

has been made by hand. (Commercial merchandise is superficial and without spirit, so avoid using or painting it.)

After you've relaxed, sent breath into your body, explored your feelings and thoughts, and meditated, allow yourself to examine the tea bowl. First, look at it on the table before you. After examining it carefully, pick it up and look at it very closely. You will notice the difference between holding and looking at the bowl in your hands and looking at it from a distance. This is important, because to paint something requires a sense of close relationship to it, whether through visualization or actual contact, or both.

Beginning with sight, activate your five senses to explore the tea bowl. Find its sound, taste, and smell as well as its feel and appearance. Close your eyes now and touch it again; smell it, listen to it. Put the bowl down, and keeping your eyes closed, imagine that you still see the tea bowl before you. Imagine you go toward it, slowly becoming smaller as you approach it, until its size becomes the universe for you. Float inside, to the center. Imagine yourself gradually merging into that center until you enter the spirit of the tea bowl, become the tea bowl itself. Become conscious of your new shape, texture, color, and design. Perhaps one sense will seem more real to you than others, and this will allow you to enter more fully into the nature and spirit of your bowl. Can you feel the shape of your inner space, your unique markings and lines? Try to feel your weight: are you heavy or light? Can you sense whether you are transparent or opaque? Where is your center?

Still a tea bowl, turn outward now; look around and see where you are. Can you look back at your "original" self, sitting with your eyes closed, meditating? Look at the other objects on the table. Notice that you can see beneath the table, even into other rooms if you want. You may even imagine the places you've been, the uses you've been put to, the hands that have held you, the tea fragrances that have warmed you.

Whenever you feel ready to return to your own body you may say good-bye to your tea bowl, taking its essence with you.

Slowly open your eyes. You will now know from the inside what makes your tea bowl different from all other tea bowls. And you will also know why you cannot paint simply by copying pictures or even by copying "reality." Reality is a little different from what our eyes alone would have us think.

Orchid Meditation

The experience of painting from direct contact with nature or in the presence of an actual subject is important, but not always accessible. The last meditation was designed to guide your seeing "inside" the tea cup and even your "becoming" this magical object, so enabling you to see beneath a table and even into other rooms. You don't need direct contact to become the subject you wish to paint. Looking is only one way to become famil-

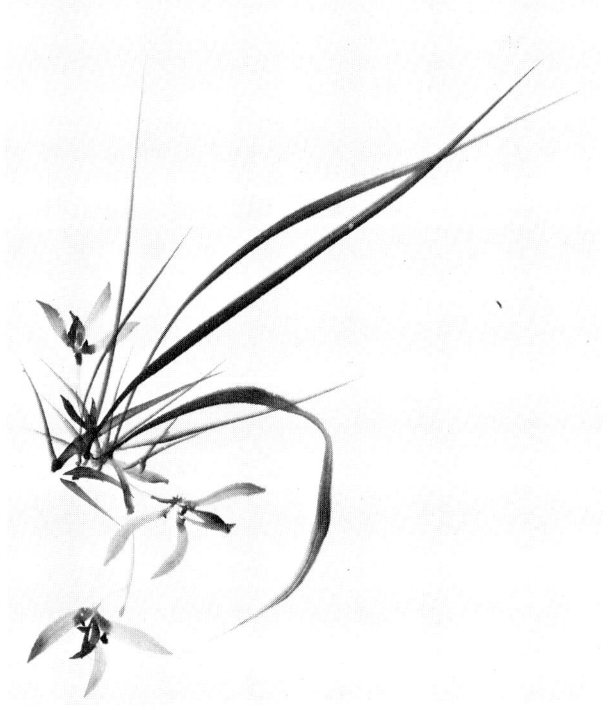

Near the Waterfall. These orchids are growing from an overhang, but the overhang is left to the imagination. There are a number of things to notice here: the subtle shading of the petals from dark at the tips to light grey at the center, the way the leaves turn up at the ends, the striation in the bottom leaf, and the relatively restrained number of elements.

iar with a subject. You can journey inside to
learn about a subject such as orchids.

Japanese orchids are flowers you may be familiar with, though they grow in the damp mountain-
ous reaches of Japan and China. The Japanese
(and Chinese) have a special way of painting orchids, as you can see from "Near the Waterfall,"
on page 28. Before you paint orchids, let's visit
an orchid where it grows.

After the basic centering exercise, relaxing and
breathing into your body, close your eyes and
imagine you are traveling to a warm country to go
into the mountains to look at orchids. Now you
are on the trail, climbing into a high valley. There
is vegetation everywhere, and it is quite humid and
warm. You are walking next to a stream, up toward a small waterfall. It is a steamy, hot place
that grows cool and breezy near the waterfall's
mist. At the waterfall, along the sides of the chasm,
orchids are growing out of the rock face. The
sturdy leaves sway languidly in the gentle breeze,
the flowers droop with dew. The colors are vivid.

Picking out an orchid plant you feel attracted
to, examine it carefully. Look at it, smell it, feel
the wet leaves, taste the fresh crispness, notice how
the leaves bend and flow despite their strength.

Closing your eyes, let yourself merge with the
orchid; become the orchid. Feel your long wet
leaves, feel the delicacy of your flowers, see the
soft coloring and the translucent petals. Your
roots reach down between the rocks, holding your
body strongly in place. The rocks are secure. The
waterfall, the flowers and vegetation, the mist and
dew, permeate your days, nights, and mornings.
You can feel your leaves gently moving in the
breeze, your flowers nodding, strength and beauty
both within you.

When you are ready, say good-bye to your
flower and return to your body, descend the
mountain, remember what your room is like and
where you really are. When you want, you can
open your eyes slowly, but do not try to "see"
anything. Allow the visions to unfold themselves
through your brush.

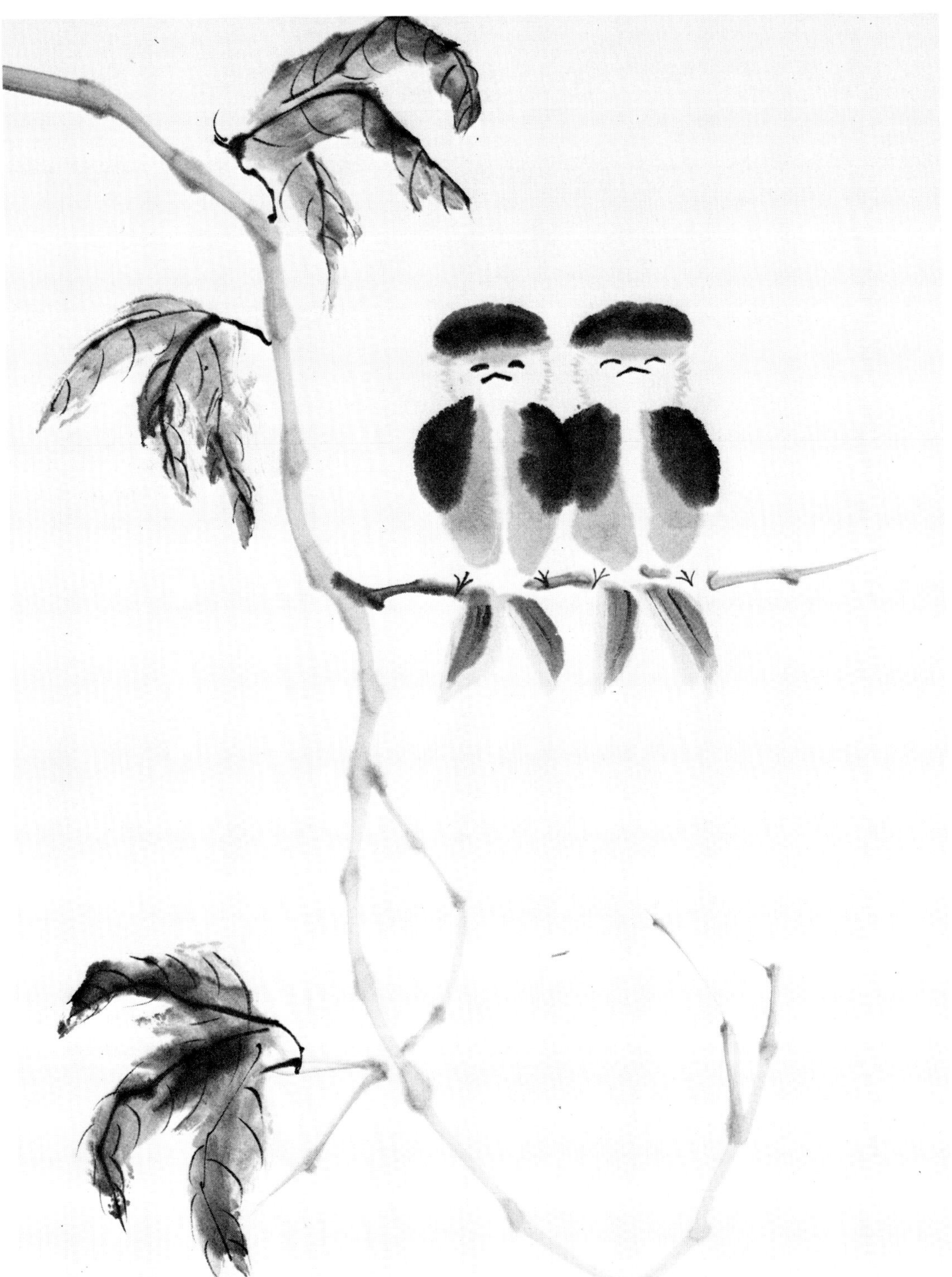

Waiting for Spring. The birds were painted first, using a wet brush; the facial details were added after the ink had dried a little, otherwise the beak and eyes would have blurred. The lighter grey was put down first, and the darker color added on top before the grey dried, so the two colors blended somewhat. The leaves were made with a three-ink brush of medium wetness. The leaf veins were drawn in with a very fine brush.

In a Bird's Eye

A bamboo grove hibernates quietly beneath a
layer of snow. Or it is tossed by the wind and
rain on a stormy night. Two artists can paint the
same scene, yet one painting will appear sad and
lonely, the other fresh and lively. People, plants,
animals, and landscapes are the flesh of sumi-e.
Parts of things — a branch and a few blossoms,
a pair of hands, the reflection in a pond, or the
abstract shadows of a forest or cityscape — can
also be paintings. Human interactions, humorous or sad, loving or angry, can easily become
paintings once we begin to see them that way.
Attributed to animals, these human qualities take
on a more subjective quality, and may become
allegorical or symbolic, humorous or fantastic.

How we view the things we paint — people, animals, landscapes, events, the interactions of the
world — depends on many things. Objects and
events have a certain reality and truth, of course.
Faces tend to be round, branches are connected
to the earth, houses have walls, birds have wings,
and so on. Yet we each have a unique way of
seeing these things.

At different times we will see the same thing
differently. Our vision is constantly in a state of
flux and change, as our feelings and thoughts
change. Similarly, our bamboos will be tossed by
inner winds as well as by the winds of the world.
The human faces we paint will reveal our joy as
well as theirs, our sadness as well as theirs. As
for the humorous expression in a bird's eye, that
will be ours alone.

Our senses and our feelings are the paths to
knowing what we paint, whether we paint from
"life," from "pictures," or from "fantasy." Our
senses and our feelings both connect us with and
separate us from the world. While painting pine,
we feel its stubborn, rough and pointy growth.
Painting bamboo, we feel its wet coolness, its
resilient strength. Painting a bird, we feel its

Stormy Night. Bamboo is often
drawn tossed by stormy winds.
Though the leaves cross each other,
they all blow in the same direction.
The darker leaves were painted
first.

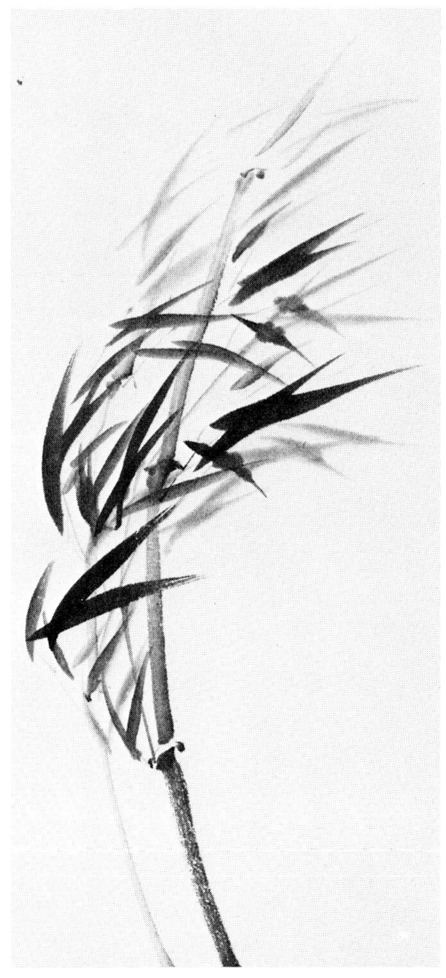

nervous alertness, its body warmth. Painting a
flower, we smell its fragrance. Everywhere we see
beauty and perfection. And if we listen closely,
we can even hear the sound of the mountain.

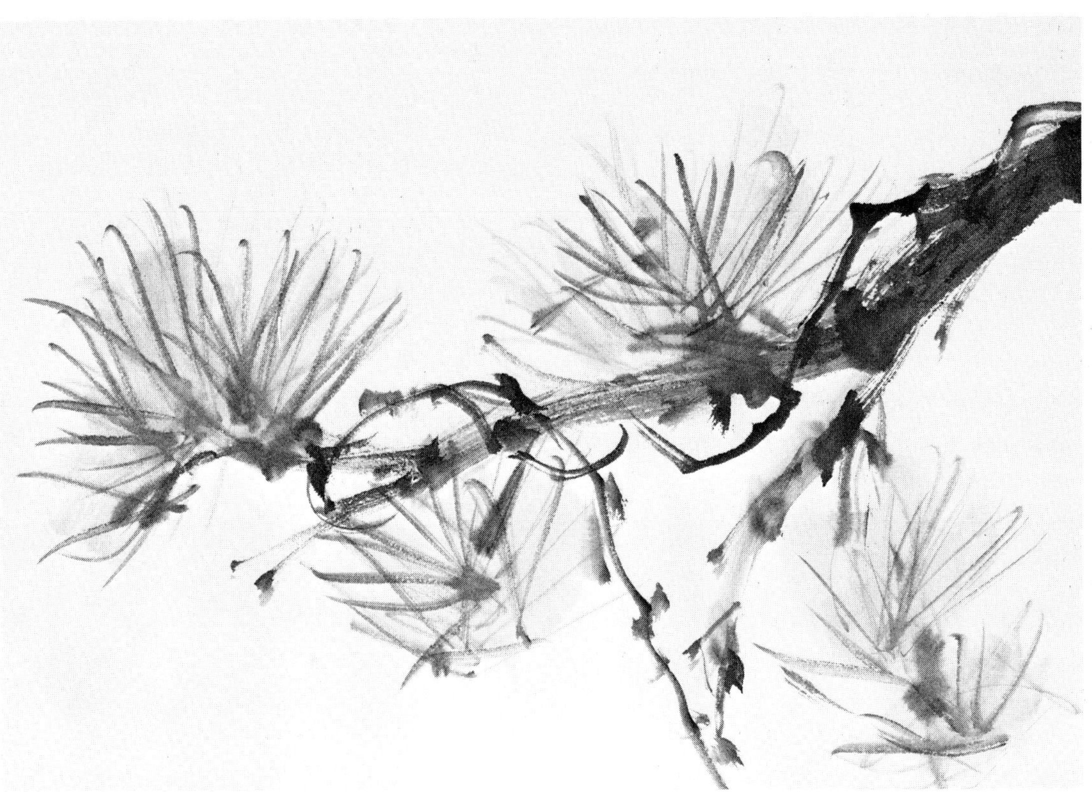

Pine. This painting was purposely
rough in execution. The branch
was painted first with a dry brush.
After the needles were drawn, a
light wash was added to lend depth.

FOLLOW THE BRUSH

Art is valued highly because it requires many skills. It is most valued by those who do it. Acquiring these skills is a challenging, exciting experience because it asks you to pay attention to what is happening to you every moment you paint. Paying attention includes focusing on your breathing, observing your senses, feelings, thoughts, identifying with the object you are painting, and following the interaction between the inner and the outer paintings. Painting with this kind of awareness is enlivening — it gives life.

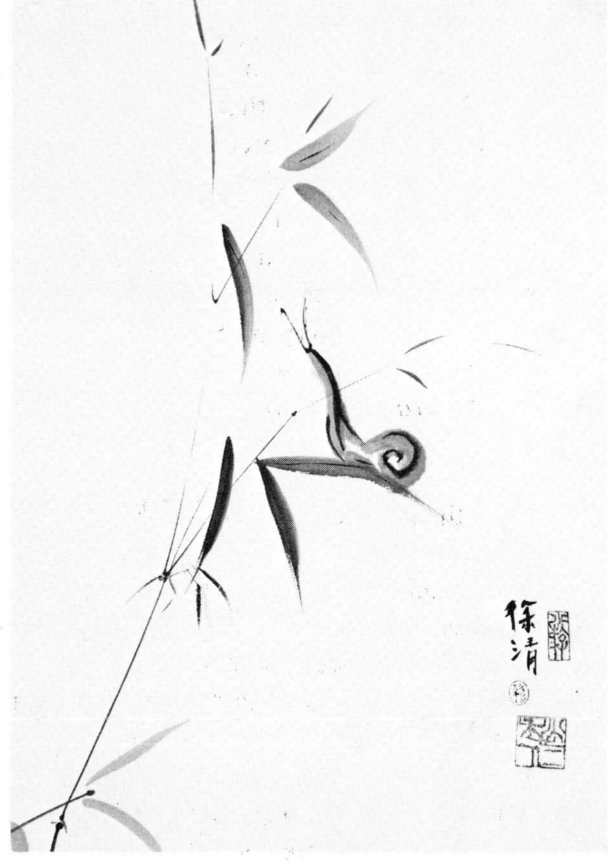

Hungry Snail.

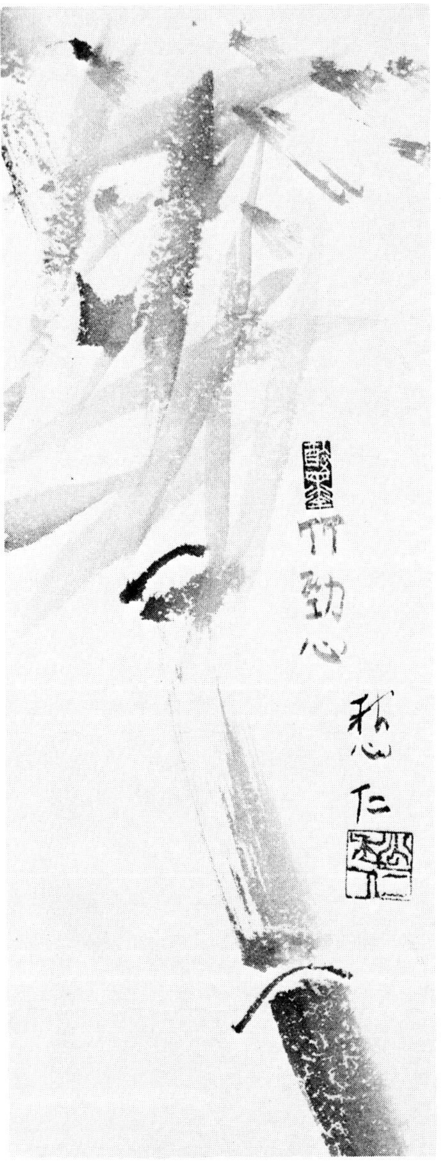

Splashed Leaves. This was done rapidly with little attention to detail. The abstract elements are numerous. Although not painted with a single brush stroke, there is a consistency of style that gives the painting a unified feeling.

The meditations of Chapter Three are designed to be used before you pick up the brush. The meditations in this chapter are done with brush in hand. Practically speaking, the exercises in this section are intended to introduce you to some different "ways" of painting. Ideally, they will build upon your own unique approach to painting, and will increase your inner knowledge.

Painting is actually a poem constructed from the prose of daily life. It is a kind of shorthand that is available to you simply by your paying attention to the flow and flux of each day. Learning how to paint is a process of learning about yourself. The joys are numberless, and barriers exist only as long as you fail to see they are the path.

There is an old saying, "Everything conspires to hinder artistic creation." This may be an overstatement. No one can deny the constant presence of disruptive elements, ranging from the ringing of the telephone to the ringing in your head. But to be aware of them is to diminish their power; to deal with them is to realize that they are not you. The very weaknesses you perceive in yourself, those you are most self-critical of, may be the building blocks of your personal skills and resources. A Zen paradox states, "For everything that is true, its opposite is also true." Thus we turn the tables: As "everything conspires to hinder artistic creation," so, too, "Everything conspires *toward* artistic creation."

Painting with One Brush Stroke

We live in a society whose abundance allows us often to substitute things for real wants and needs. How many times do we cram our bellies to stuff our loneliness? How many homes are overfull of gadgets and furniture?

As in our social habits, we have a tendency to overpaint, to overfill the paper well after the painting has made its statement. Remember, the

painting is your meditation room: if you do not
clutter it, it will exhale air and light. The quality
and interest of the painting depends on the few,
not the many, things it contains.

Begin this exercise by taking one brush stroke
for a walk. Just move the brush across the paper,
as if you were walking next to it, and feel what
its life is like. Then let *it* take *you* for a walk.
Let the brush lead the way across the paper. Feel
what the brush knows and what it can do. Feel
the paper with your brush; respond to those things
the brush knows more about than you — the texture, the wetness, the ink charge, and so on.
While you must have control of the brush to paint,
the brush has a life of its own.

Many of my students try to look at what they
are painting as they are moving the brush across
the paper. This is like trying to watch your feet
while dancing. It cannot be done. While you
should "know" what you are painting, it is best
to "forget" what you are painting until you fin-
ish it. Avoid the tendency to try to see whether
the painting looks the way it is "supposed to."
Trying to judge the outer painting while in the
midst of it interrupts the rhythm and flow of the
inner painting. Allow the brush stroke to paint
itself without your trying to interrupt. If you
take the attitude of never having seen a brush
stroke before, watching one appear on the paper
will be an exciting experience. The true beginner is always surprised at the universe. May we
always be beginners!

Practice single lines first, long and short, thin
and heavy, wavy and straight. Then move on to
circles, trying all the variations you can discover.
Explore pages of squiggles and scratches. Practice,
move, explore, discover, and begin again.

Because sumi-e uses a kind of shorthand, an entire painting may contain very few strokes. Nothing is painted over. Subtle effects of volume and
depth are created largely with a single stroke
through techniques of shading rather than with
outlines or multiple layers of ink. Thus an orchid

A Study of Lines. The brush is a remarkably versatile tool, able to create broad variations of texture, color, and thickness. Practicing the strokes and lines shown here will give you facility and allow you to discover what you and your brush are capable of. The long squiggly line in the center was made with black ink on only one side of the brush. The large smoky line near the bottom, unlike the rest, uses the side of the brush as well as the tip.

Heavenly Jewel. Although circular in form, these lines are painted primarily with the tip of the brush. The smoky lines begin to use more of the side of the brush. This is good practice for learning how to twist the brush, because the circle is made in one stroke without lifting the brush from the paper. To keep the hairs in line, the brush has to be slowly twisted in your fingers as you make the circle. In traditional instruction, this is one of the first subjects assigned.

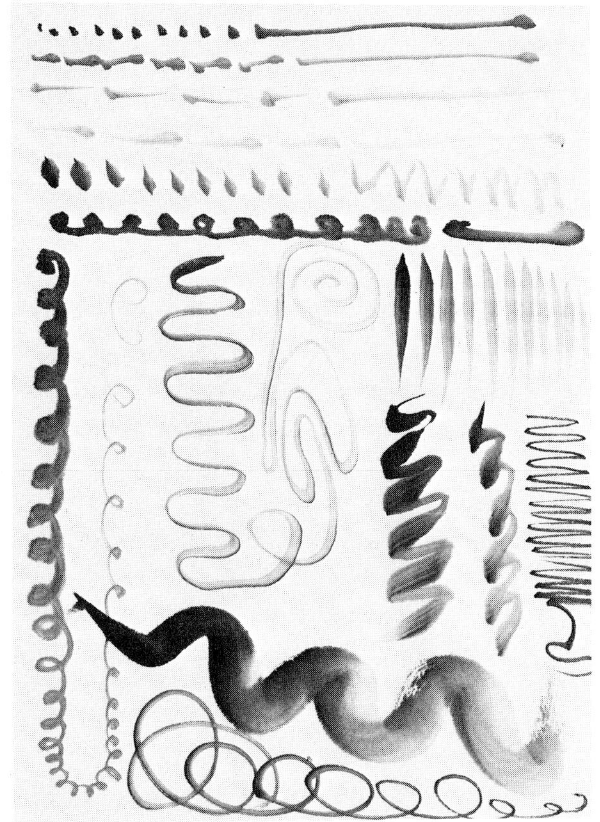

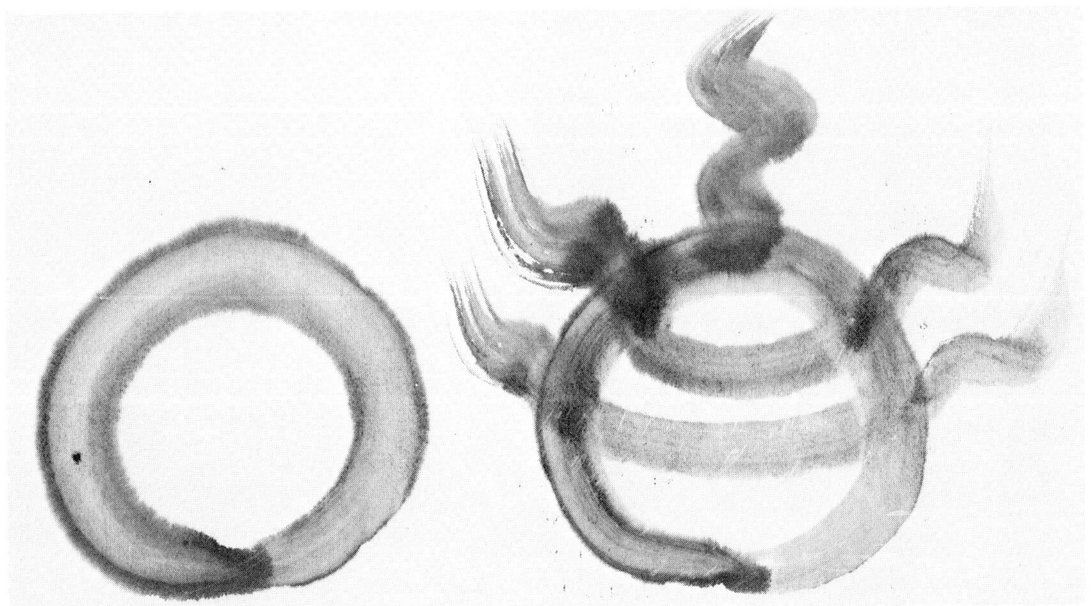

leaf is painted with a single narrow stroke. So,
too, a bamboo leaf. A bamboo stalk may consist
of three or four sections, each of which is a single
wide brush stroke. (To help you understand and
practice these single strokes, turn for a moment
to the instruction section in Chapter Six, pages
64 to 78, which explains how to paint bamboo
and orchid.)

A stroke is like a breath. Each orchid leaf, each
bamboo leaf, each section of the bamboo stalk,
can be painted with one exhalation. Several
strokes may be grouped together and painted in
one breath. Often, five or six or more bamboo
leaves are painted all at once, in one exhalation.
The leaves of the plant will appear less scattered
and more connected, because they will have a
unity of life energy as well as a unity of execution and color. Similarly, the separate sections
of a bamboo stalk are painted in one exhalation.
Your breath becomes the generating force that
gives a unified life energy to the bamboo stalk.
Rather than having five separate strokes, you will
have a living plant!

A sumi-e painting is actually one breath, one
stroke. Of course, one stroke in this sense does
not mean, literally, a single touching of brush and

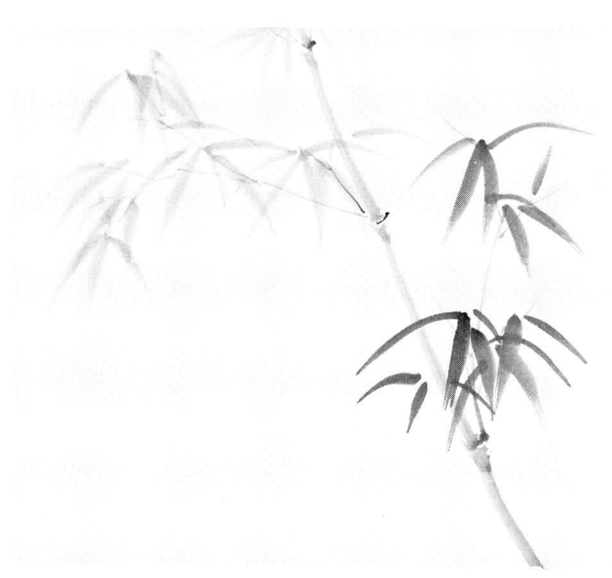

Wet Bamboo. The mood and coloring of this bamboo is monochromatic, made with a limited number
of strokes of a similar style. After
painting the bole of the bamboo
(in medium grey, with the joints in
darker grey), the leaves can all be
painted with one brush load of ink,
beginning with the darker leaves at
bottom, then the leaves above, then
moving up to the gradually lighter
greys of the upper branches, and
finishing with the almost invisible
leaves near the top. As with most
bamboo, the bole and the smaller
stems were painted first, and the
leaves afterwards. Notice that all
the leaves are of a similar size and
style.

ink to paper. A painting is a single stroke in the sense that it is a unified whole, both in spirit and execution. Be aware of the unity of what you are painting. Painting with a single stroke, a single breath, imparts the breath of life to your painting. Your painting will leap to life before you.

Paint without Paper

We are always painting. If we had brushes attached to our hands, we would inadvertently, by the natural grace of our movements, create masterpieces of visual motion. Observe yourself in daily motion — flicking crumbs off a table, swirling a mop on the floor. A brush stroke begins at one end of the universe and ends at the other, just as your

The Elements. A copy of an ancient masterpiece, this painting contains all the basic elements of bamboo — shoots, stalks, leaves. Yet the artist is more concerned with creating an abstract pattern in two dimensions than a realistic three-dimensional "illusion."

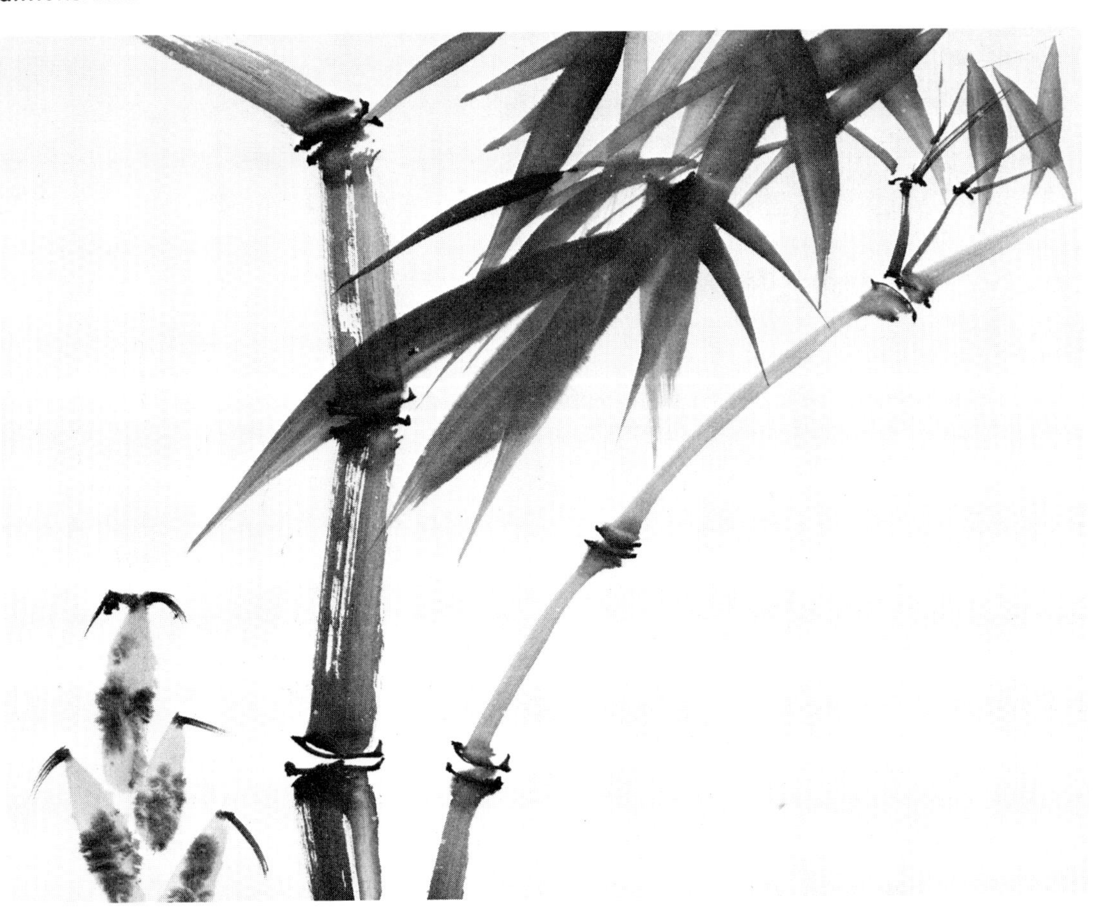

washing and sweeping motions do. So when you
paint sumi-e, do not paint as if the painting were
separate from you.

Many of my students begin painting when the
brush touches the paper and stop painting when
the brush leaves the paper. This produces chop-
py, lifeless lines. There is no acknowledgment of
the world beyond the edge of the paper, no energy
pointing to the rest of the universe, of which the
painting is only a part.

Like this type and these words, a bamboo leaf
begins far ahead of its visual record on the paper,
and like our memory of the words that create
sentences and activities, it ends long after it dis-
appears into the whiteness of space. The energy
of a bamboo stalk projects far beyond the two or
three sections we see. The smallest leaf contains
the energy of an entire plant. Each stroke in
your bamboo painting should contain the essence
of bamboo. If it is a big bamboo, the two or
three boles painted should express the energy of
a sixty-foot plant. If you paint only a few leaves,
they should convey the feeling of all the leaves in
the entire grove.

When we paint, our brushes are moving all the
time. The motion begins in space and ends there.
It is only incidental that the stroke touches the
paper. Our paper is only two dimensions. Yet it
expresses the depth and vitality of three dimensions, plus time, and it must express everything
that is off the edge of the paper, too. If we paint
as if the world existed in two dimensions, our
paintings will be flat and lifeless. We must paint
in three dimensions in order to distill the essence
of the boundless universe onto a flat surface.

Paint Rhythmically

There is a rhythm to painting, particularly to painting sumi-e. Maintaining the proper tension to complete a painting in one brush stroke, one breath, is
a part of that rhythm. The parts of a unified
whole are measured out in a rhythm. A compari-

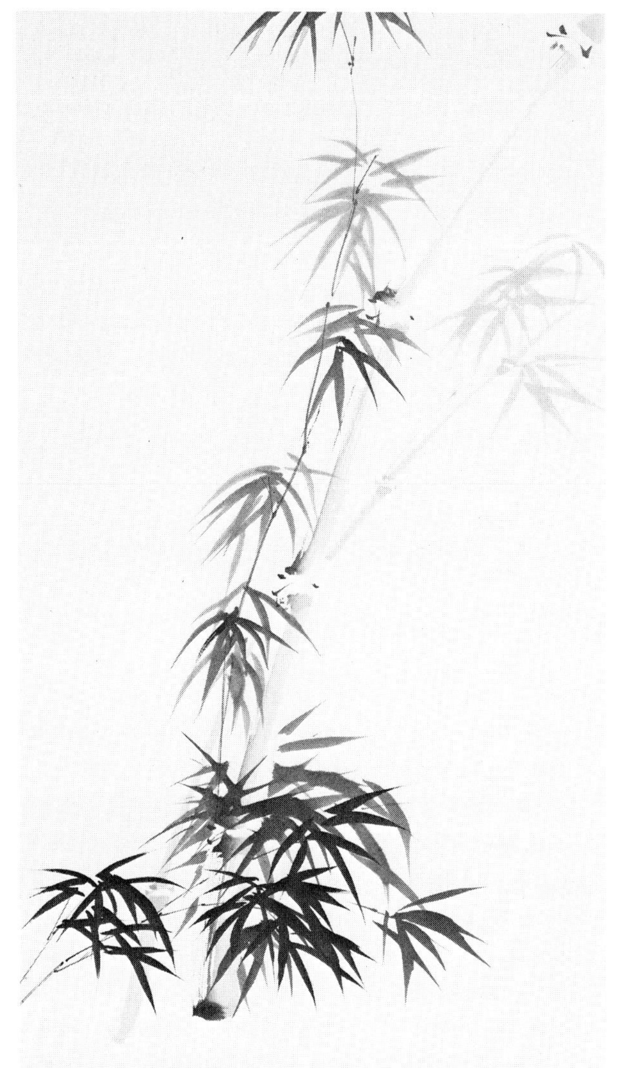

son with another activity will help clarify what I mean.

There is a rhythm to playing tennis. The ball is hit back and forth with grace and regularity. An alert tennis player, taking cues from the opponent's body, begins running to where the ball will be even before the other player hits it there. The rhythm of a good player has such flexibility that it gives ultimate control of the game. It is the strength of this rhythm that determines where the ball will be. When a good player swings in rhythm, the ball has no choice but to be there.

40

Sumi-e is painted with a rhythm similar to that of a tennis player. The way bamboo is painted is a good example. The separate sections of the stalk are painted one after another, forming a unified plant with a rhythmic flow. The leaves are painted with a rhythm, also. They are painted in groups, all with the same feel and flow to them.

Just as a tennis player winds up before hitting the ball and follows through after hitting it, a painter begins and ends each stroke far beyond the confines of the page. A paint brush is like a tennis racquet; all we feel is the hit of the ball against the racquet, all we see is the stroke on the page. But the energy behind both is powerful. Done in rhythm, the strokes create a ballet.

Use Up All the Paper at One Sitting

In some traditional styles of painting, oils, for example, it is usual to spend time working and re-working one painting. The spirit of sumi-e is more spontaneous than that. Care and planning are needed before the brush ever touches the paper. Before painting, decide what you want to paint, and then execute it with a rhythm that is appropriate to your mood and to the mood of the painting. A painting should take no more than a few minutes. Some more elaborate or detailed paintings may take as long as ten minutes, but very few. Bamboo and orchid are quick; pine and plum take longer. Some detailed landscapes can take hours, of course, but that is really a different kind of painting. (See, for example, "Autumn Mountains," on page 10.)

Choosing a simple subject, set yourself a goal of using thirty, fifty, a hundred sheets of paper at one sitting. You may paint the same composition repeatedly; you may vary it; you may paint the parts; you may practice different things over and over. Do not, however, dwell on one painting. If you lift your brush from the paper, if you find yourself wondering what to add to it — then it is time to move on to the next sheet. Don't worry

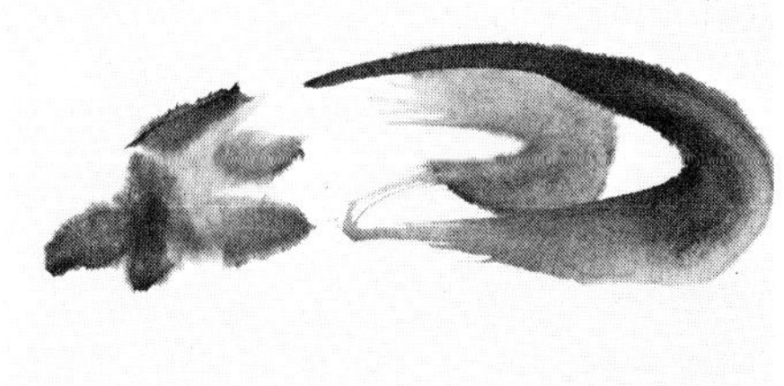

Eggplant. Common fruits and vegetables, available year round, are good subjects, providing a variety of shapes, colors, and textures for practice.

about wasting paper. One purpose of this exercise is to learn how to feel comfortable wasting paper. If it takes one hundred sheets of paper to produce one painting you love, the ninety-nine misses are but steppingstones to that achievement.

Painting Sky, Snow, and Sea

Learn to paint the difficult, sometimes the unimaginable — the surface of a pond, a clear bottle against a white wall, the sound of falling snow. Learn how to make a dry branch, a luxuriant leaf, to show roundness and three dimensions on the flat surface of whiteness. And each time you learn something new, repeat it, so that you can do it at will. When you achieve the effect of a fish in water, do not rest content. Paint it again the next day. Luck contributes to discovery, but it has no bearing on skill. After you repeat it again and again, then you can forget you know it. At the moment that you need to create a transparent surface, no thinking will be necessary. With a child's innocence you will surprise yourself with what you already know.

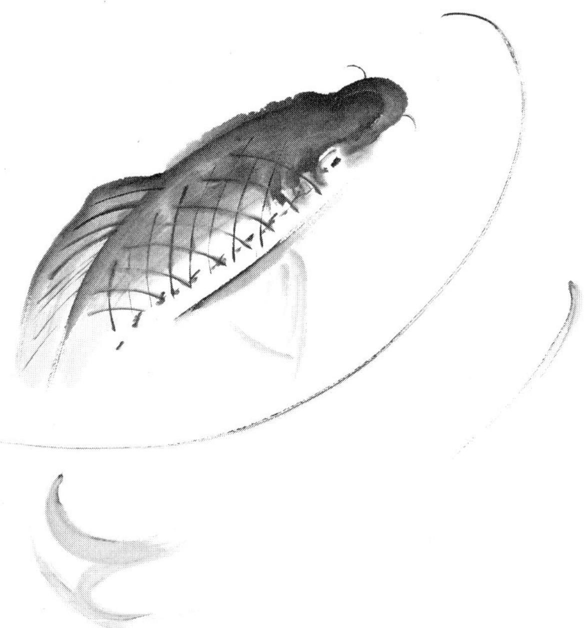

Carp. Water, glass, snow, and other difficult subjects are painted as often by lines as by means of shading. Do not be too quick to paint in a surface with a wash. The white of your paper has a tangible surface already.

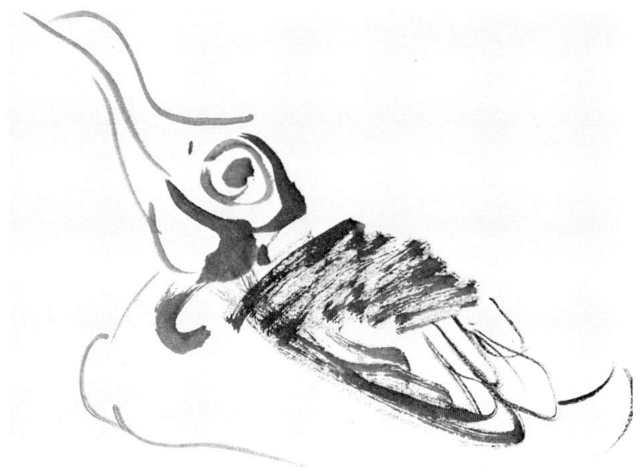

Quack. A "terrible painting." By following the instructions, "Take the subject you are working on and paint it as fast as you can, making as many mistakes as possible, making the worst painting possible," Janet Biehl surprised herself with this eye-catching duck.

Make the Worst Painting You Can Imagine

I have discovered that people are the worst judges of their own paintings, but make accurate observations about other people's paintings. Therefore, this exercise is done best with other people, and the more, the merrier. Simply pick an object that attracts you and try to paint it as badly as you can. Do not try to paint a square if you are looking at a circle. Paint the object itself. But simply forget trying to make it look the way it is "supposed" to look. Let go and let your brush do the painting.

Does this seem like an odd exercise? Most of my students think that until they discover that their "worst" paintings draw unexpected admiration and favorable comments about their flow, freedom, and accurate expression of the object they are intended to represent. But you must try this exercise in order to know for yourself.

Painting Parts

Sumi-e captures the spirit of its subject in a few strokes. This spirit is alive in all parts of any subject, and paintings often disclose only a small part, a leaf or a twig, a few flowers, a single bird. As the painter, you wish to distill the essence of your subject into a few strokes that express its spirit, feeling, or character.

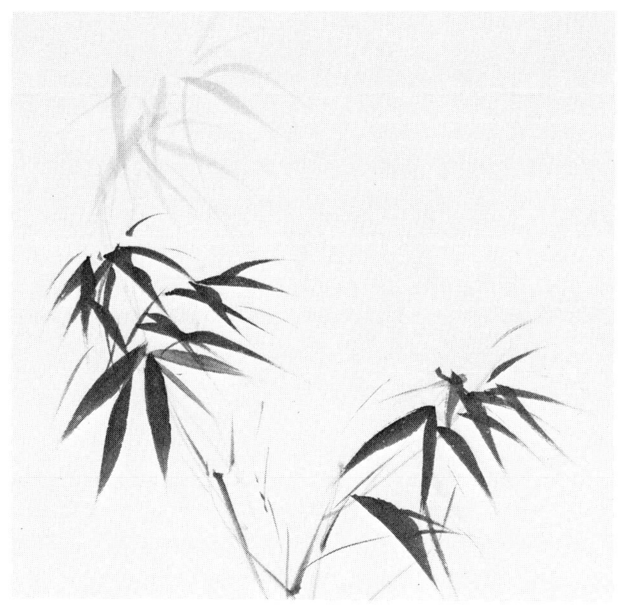

Painting a part of a subject requires focusing on
the essential part. The subject evokes a feeling,
and this is the key to what you paint and how you
paint it. Of course you may as easily start with a
feeling and then find a subject. Most paintings
are a combination of both.

Moods and feelings are best expressed with
plants like bamboo, pine, and so on, rather than
animals. Animals best express particular character
traits like humor or wisdom. To paint, it is necessary to "become" whatever you paint or to discover its essential characteristic. Your meditations
will help you approach any painting always with
the object of discovering the most essential part
or aspect of your subject. What you ultimately
include or exclude will articulate the depth of
your involvement and perspective.

Meditating on whatever you are feeling produces
memories and images from which you may draw
your paintings. A memory of a beautiful sunny
day in the woods will lead you to paint with that
mood invigorating the work. It is essential, however, to discover what particular aspect of your
subject best expresses that mood or feeling. It
may be a flower, a few branches on a tree, one

shoot of bamboo, a bird, or a spring landscape. Paint the minimum that is necessary to express the feeling; this will produce the most involving and exciting pictures. Aim for spareness. Let the empty space speak.

Animals can be a wonderful expression of particular human qualities. Are you feeling strong, foolish, wise? For any aspect of the human condition, meditate upon what animal best embodies this characteristic. Or you can assign this characteristic to an animal, since the animal world is about as versatile as the human when it comes to varieties of behavior. Again, it is essential to discover within yourself the animal's "center," that part which embodies the animal's spiritual force, such as the spine of a cat, the stomach of a cow, the head of a bird. It is important that you get in touch with the central quality of your cat or bird. Then you will perceive what makes it different from all other cats and birds.

Your plants, too, are equally alive and depend upon sympathetic vibrations for their nurturance, for their life and growth on the white space of your paper. To paint a plant you must feel what it is like to be the plant. Find what part of yourself is curved with vines and tendrils, the

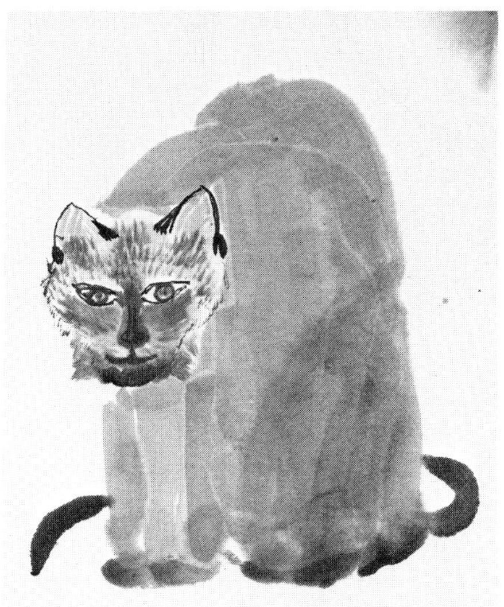

Sphinx. The face is quite detailed; the body washed in. The shadows on the face suggest the shadowy nature of the cat, even though it seems to be smiling.

Cat and Mouse. The character of the cat is expressed in its entire being, but the chest and front leg best express the tension in the painting. Notice the free brushwork, the contrast of wet and dry, and the lack of detail.

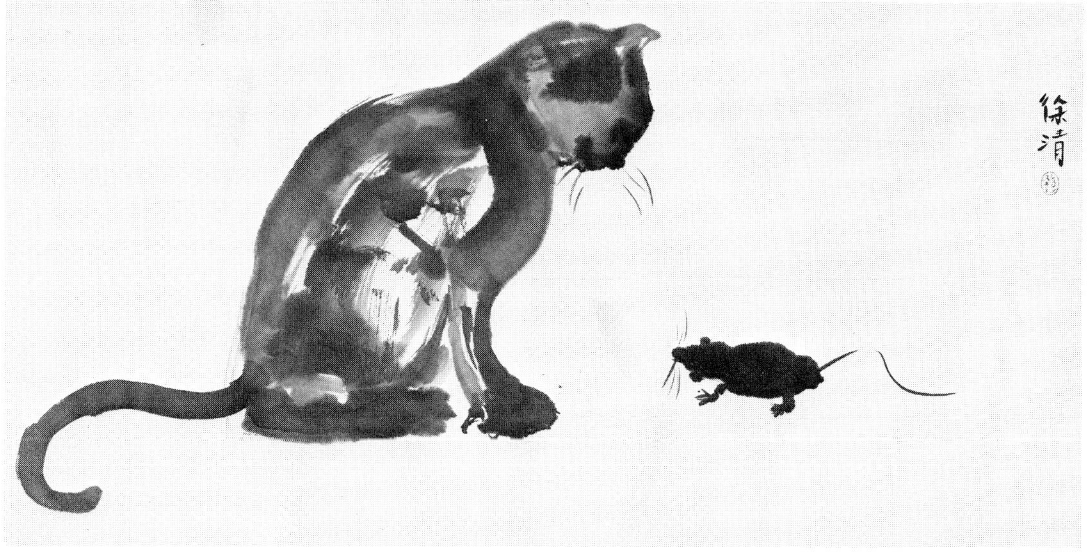

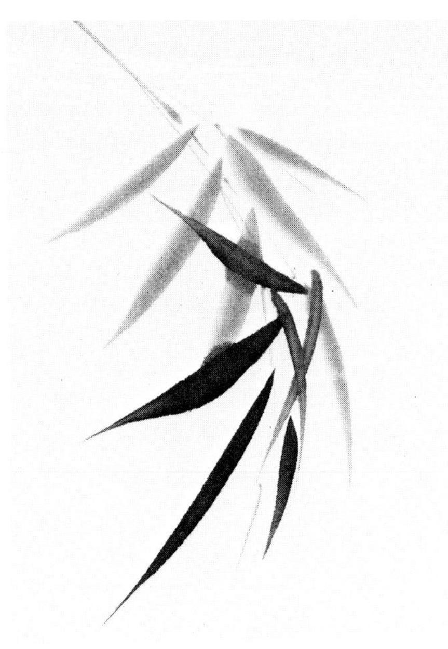

roots unmovingly anchored in the earth of your body and the leaves and flowers reaching like your arms and head out to the universe. Let your brush vitalize that plant in the language of sumi-e.

Once you have discovered the most vital part, focus upon its moving force, and allow the painting to unfold. It is preferable to narrow the subject down to the single image that most perfectly expresses the desired mood. Most paintings are of one or two animals or plants, or even a single branch, leaf, or bird. Learn to trust your own meditations and feelings to extract that image. Your painting is a distillation — the earth in a carrot leaf, the sky in a sparrow's outspread wing.

Additional Meditations

The following are additional meditations for your mind and brush. Like a painting, you may flesh them out as your imagination suggests.

Blind Seeing: Using a pencil, pen or charcoal, draw on large pieces of paper with your eyes closed. First do the basic meditations, then look at something you want to paint and examine it carefully, meditatively. Then close your eyes, and as if your pencil were a finger, feel your way across the paper, painting lightly or heavily, fully

Bird in Bloom. The vital center of this bird is the stomach, although the head also contributes to its character. The beak, eye, and head were drawn first, then the body. Notice that the head is one stroke. The body also is a single stroke in which a three-ink brush was first moved right to left to form the upper chest and then, without lifting the brush from the paper, left to right to complete the lower abdomen. The beak is shaded lightly, while the rest of the bird consists largely of less refined brushwork. The branch and leaves are only roughly sketched.

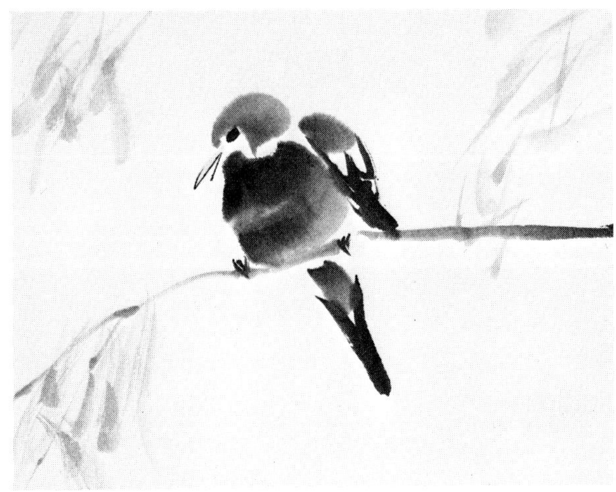

or sparsely as you visualize the memory. You may be surprised at how accurately you can see things without looking at them. You may want to extend this to painting blindly from memory things you saw yesterday, on last year's vacation, or during your childhood. And as with the orchid meditation, you can also paint blindly things you simply visualize. Music may be an additional imaginative tool.

Painting/Seeing: This meditation is done with your eyes looking only at the subject, while you paint without looking at the paper. As in the above meditation, don't worry if you go off the paper. Simply continue, or start over. After you have done this a while with pencil or pen, you may want to try it with ink and brush. The important thing is to pay attention to what you are painting, not what you have painted. Your hand and eye will find what is there, filtered through your unique personality.

The Rule of Ten: When you paint something, invoke the number 10 and decide you are going to paint the subject ten times regardless of the outcome of each separate work. You may use separate sheets of paper, or you may put all ten on one sheet if the sheet is large enough or the subject small enough. The long rolls of paper are useful for this exercise. As you paint, you will be able to stop worrying about each separate work because you will be making ten different paintings. Another discovery will be that each painting is different, and that they usually improve as your knowledge increases. In addition to painting something ten times, try painting ten things once, paint the same subject ten ways, and paint ten subjects the same way. This "short" exercise may take time to do, but you will learn a great deal about how to paint.

Copying: There is an old saying, "Copy everyone, imitate no one." Much can be learned by copying the great painters of the past and present. But remember that the way of these painters was to paint from nature, from the subjects themselves. It is wise to copy them in this faithfully.

Cat on a Rock. Animals can be humorous subjects. There are many rewards in studying their movements and activities. To capture their character in a few strokes of the brush is very satisfying.

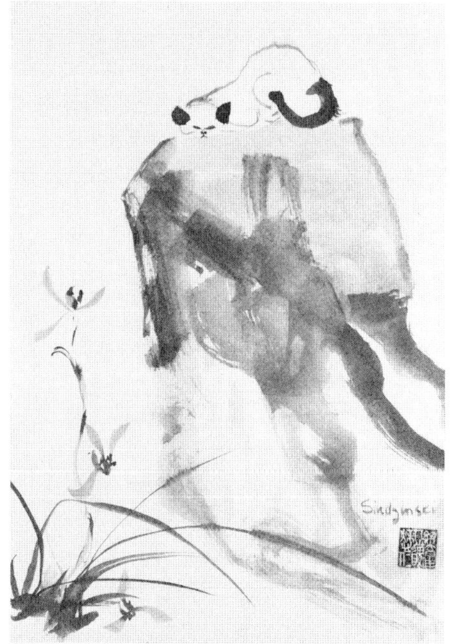

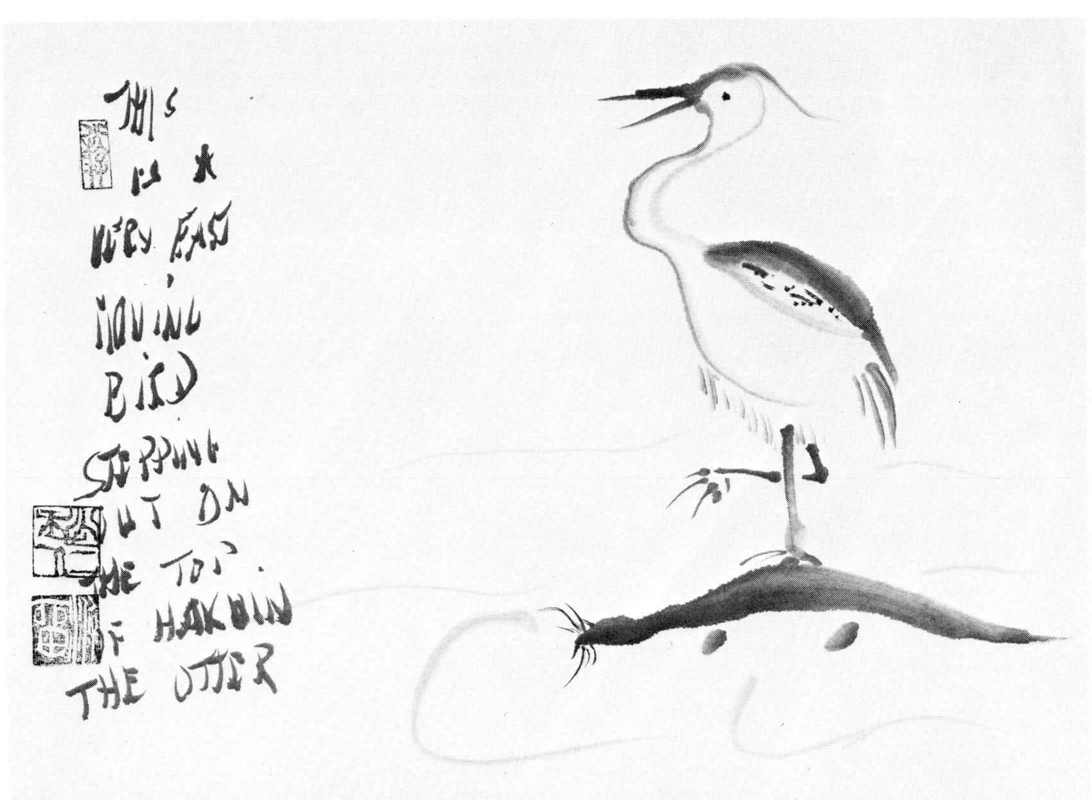

Hakuin the Otter. This painting was based on a painting by Hakuin suggested by a Zen story telling how the Buddha crossed the river to China on a bamboo leaf. Hakuin painted a heron riding on a *dojo* (a small animal living in rice fields) with an inscription saying, "What kind of character is this climbing on a person's back. The *dojo*'s bones won't stand for this, you! You [heron] have got a lot of nerve!" As Hakuin has stepped onto the back of an earlier Zen-ga tradition, so I am stepping out on top of Hakuin!

Poetry Painting: This could be called haiku painting. Haiku is the poetic equivalent of sumi-e, short poems of seventeen syllables, generally containing a single image. Ezra Pound wrote in imitation, "Faces in a subway crowd, / Petals on a wet black bough." You may use either a book of translated haiku or favorite images taken from English poetry. Using one of the meditations, translate the poetry into a painting.

There is also a tradition in Japan of illustrating stories from Zen texts. Haiga (*hai*, poetry; *ga*, painting) is a form of poetry-painting in which words and pictures are equally important elements of a unified work. In this kind of painting, even the penmanship is important to the final effect. You may want to try evoking in ink the essence of these tales or of stories of your own.

Perspective and Composition: Pictures consist of different parts or areas, and it is important that they all fit together well. This "meditation" will give you a sense of how this happens. Divide your composition into three parts: (1) perspective, (2) large forms, and (3) details. Try painting each as a separate painting. Then put them all together. In essence you are practicing parts, but the parts are structural rather than esthetic. (1) Perspective will include how everything relates in terms of size, placement, color, and so on. (2) The large forms will include the major subject of the painting and the large areas such as the white space, the space between things, and the areas inside things. (3) Details include all the "how to" elements of painting like shape, form, details of facial or structural importance, and so on.

The meditations in this chapter are all done while painting. They enable you to "pay attention" to the process which takes a painting out of the three-dimensional world we live in and brings it to life on a flat piece of paper. They are ways to experiment with both the practical and the imaginative aspects of sumi-e.

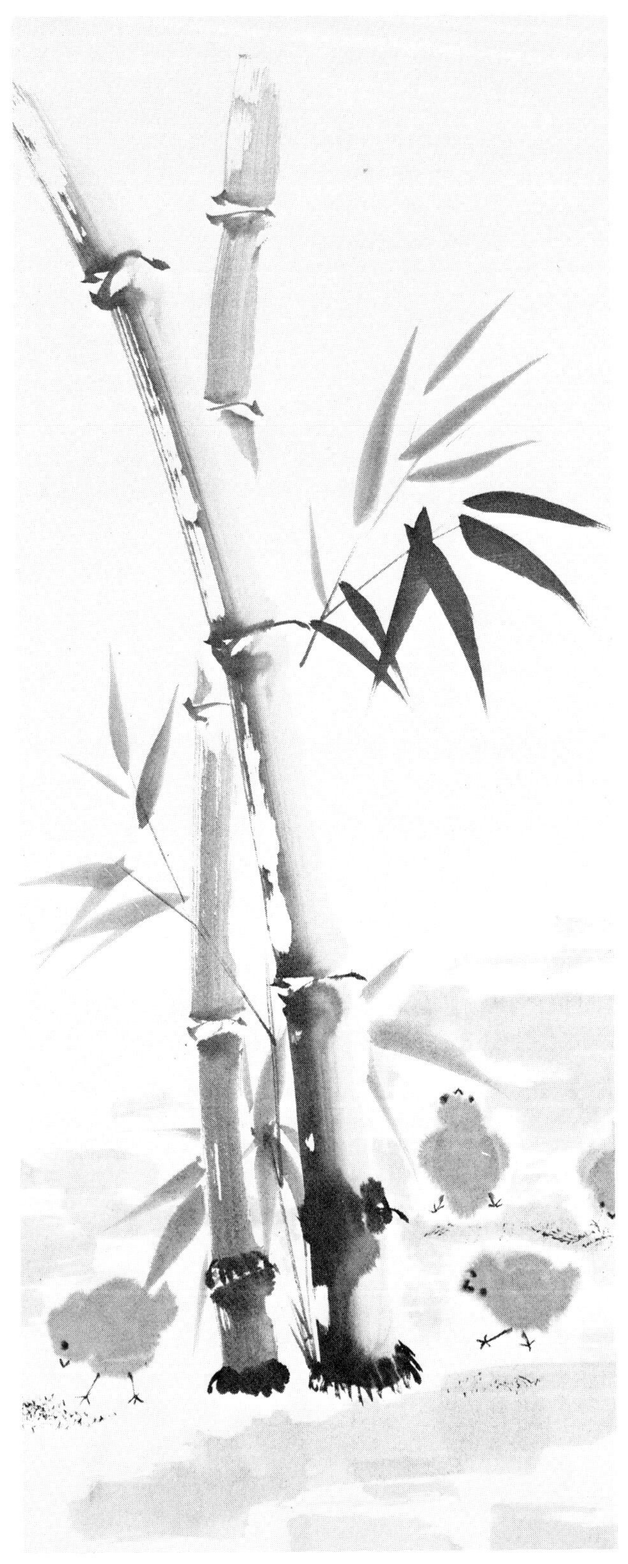

Hungry Chicks. The bamboo was painted first, and then the chicks. When painting small furry creatures it is usually better to capture their bodies first, and then to add the details of eyes and beaks.

Chapter 5

WHEN THE WELL OF INK IS THICK

"Once I'm into it I'm all right. It's the getting started that's so hard." Sound familiar? Learning something new can be as difficult as it is enjoyable, and the conflicting voices and feelings inside and outside can sometimes get the better of you. Yet feeling frustrated and confused are only stages along the road of self-discovery. Art, more than most other activities, offers you opportunities for self-discovery and self-nurturance. Because art is a process, there are stages of expansion and others of consolidation. As in life, there are times of feverish activity and times of meditative withdrawal. Both are healthy, and both are necessary.

Where and When to Paint

At home, on a train, sitting under a tree in the park, in a classroom — any place can provide an opportunity to paint. Even without brushes you

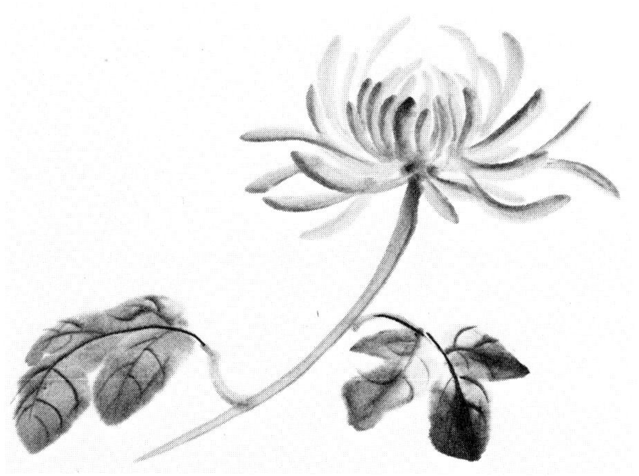

Chrysanthemum. Overall, this painting of a long-petaled chrysanthemum is soft; nothing is outlined. Shading was by means of the three-ink technique. Paint the flower, then the stem, then the leaves.

Seagulls in a Storm. In this painting, based on a sketch, the birds seem quite worried by the all-pervasive maelstrom. Beak and eye were painted before the body, and legs were added last.

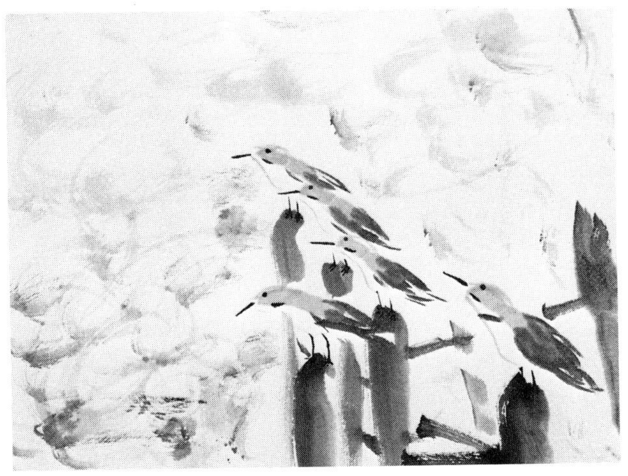

can jot down rough sketches, memory lines of the things you experience, notes on how you perceive and record. You can store mental pictures — a face here, a twig there, a flower, a bird against the grey sky, to be developed in your sketch book later. Seeing *how* you see is the first step in making a real painting.

Try painting at different times of the day, and at night. Paint in cities and in the country, indoors and out. Sketch books turn into an excellent source of new ideas, new paintings; sometimes you may want to take your brushes with you and spend a few hours or a day sitting in a grove or on a cliff overlooking a valley or in a field of flowers. And there are always people around, either to paint, to look at your painting, or to paint with you. Inevitably, anyone who is with you will wind up sketching too. If you don't talk to them, what else is there to do?

It is good to have a place to paint that you feel is yours. It may be a classroom, an art class, or your own home. Claim an easy chair, a desk, a corner of the living room, a kitchen table, anywhere so long as you feel comfortable and secure painting there.

If you have trouble finding the time to paint, try following a schedule that allows you to fit one sketch into your day. A sketch a day can be

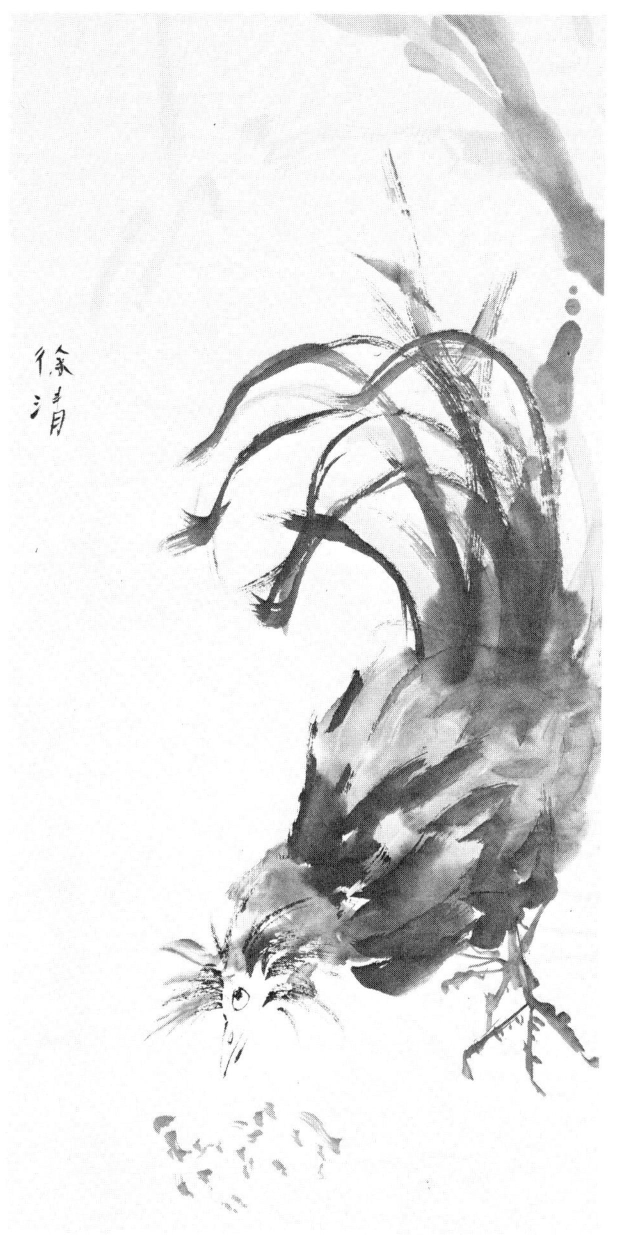

Leftover Corn. The order of painting here was beak and eyes, then head, body, feathers, and feet. The corn was added last, roughly sketched in. This painting took only a few minutes to complete.

enough to sustain the inner painter until you can get to your brushes with a longer time to paint. Sketching will probably lead you to want more, to remember how much you enjoy painting. If you let yourself nibble on a sketch a day, you will not be able to deny yourself a painting session for long.

Positions for Painting

Sitting, standing, or kneeling are positions that can be used at different times, depending on where you are and how you are feeling. There is no "proper" way to position yourself, though, traditionally, Chinese and Japanese painters use a kneeling position. This practice derives from their architecture and life style, not from any inherent virtue. The important thing is comfort, so that you are able to do what you have to do. One advantage of kneeling is that it encourages efficient breathing. It also allows easier access to large sheets of paper when you are doing a large painting. However, breathing can be just as free no matter what posture you paint in. When you are creating a large painting, standing next to a high

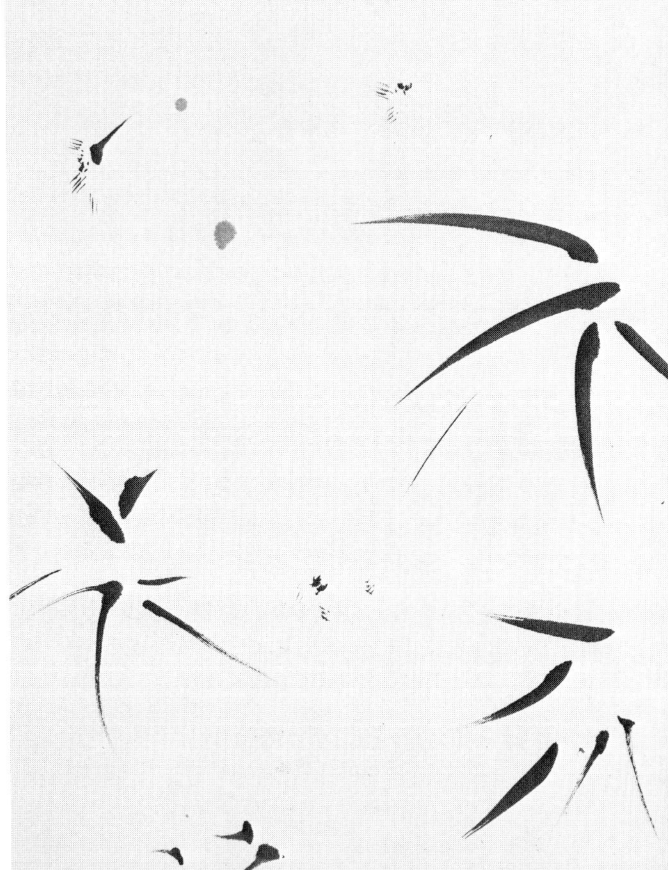

Bamboo Fantasy. This painting demonstrates the potential for abstraction in sumi-e. What began as a study of bamboo stalks became, when accidentally splattered with ink, an entirely different painting. Do not overlook the value mistakes can have.

table will enable you to reach very far, especially if you stand adjacent to the painting for the upper sections rather than attempting to reach them from the bottom.

Holding the Brush

The way the brush is held is a matter of personal preference. There is a recognized way to hold an oriental brush, but do not stop painting simply because you are not sure you have it right. The important thing to remember is that Japanese brush painting requires many variations in pressure, direction, and energy, all of which must be sensed by the fingers and the hand. So the more fingers you have on the brush, the better. Figures 1 through 6 show the traditional method of holding

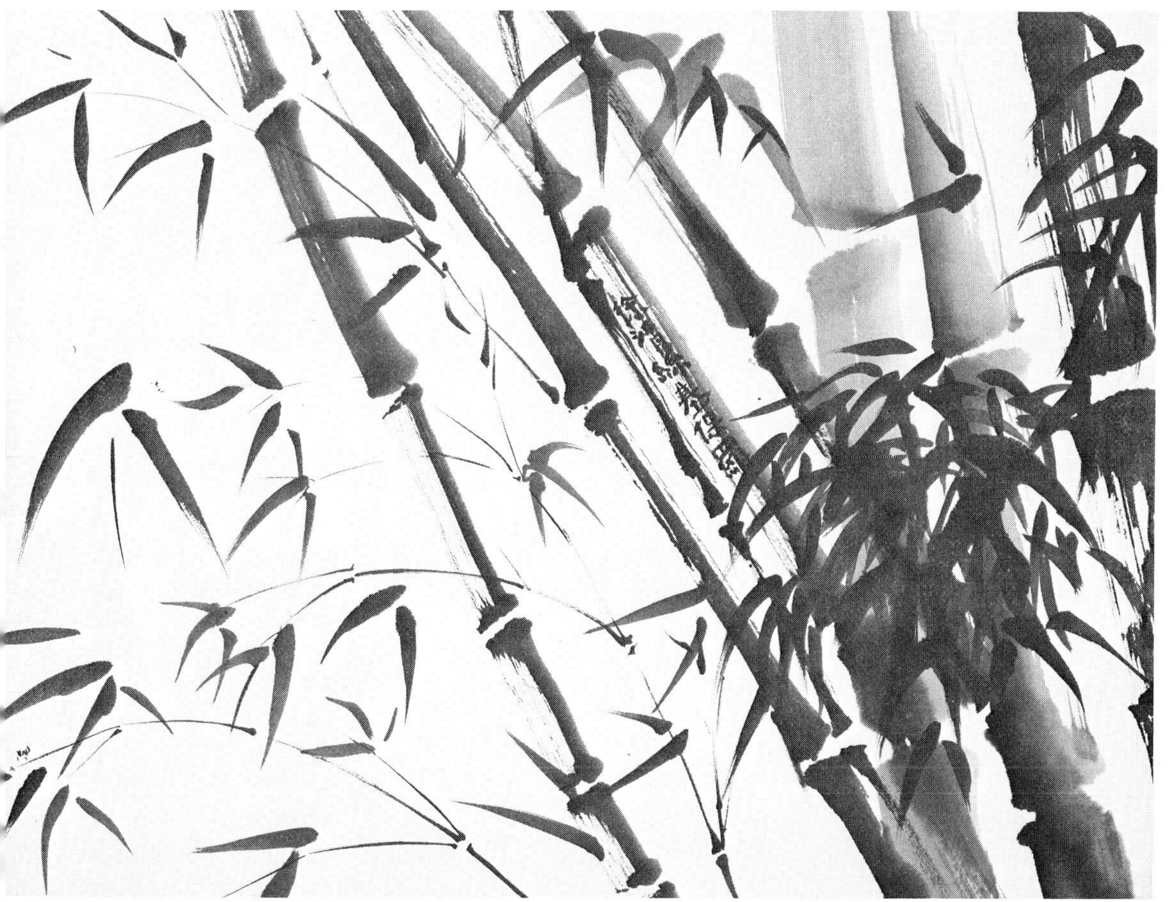

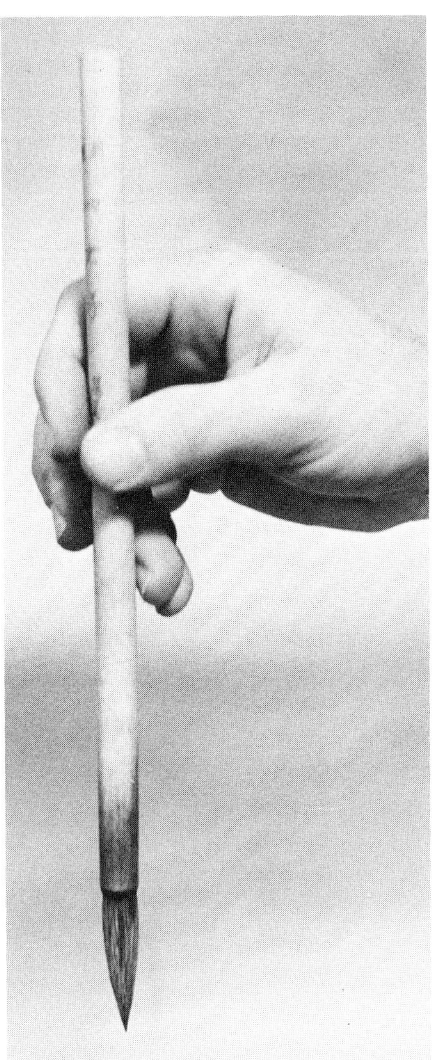

the brush in various strokes. Your thumb and first finger will oppose each other, while your second finger, placed on the same side of the brush as the first, will oppose your third finger, placed on the same side of the brush as your thumb. This will enable you to paint using only your fingers and arm, not your wrist. The wrist is always kept stiff in sumi-e painting. If you are holding the brush correctly, you should, in fact, be able to touch your wrist with the tip of your brush. Another test for the correct hold dictates that you should have enough freedom in your wrist, when holding the brush one third of the way up the handle and with your arm and wrist resting on the paper, to be able to paint a circle three or four inches in diameter. When trying this, hold your brush as vertical as possible. If you are only able to make a one-inch circle, then you may be holding the brush like a pencil, at too extreme an angle. The brush is never held like a pencil, an ice pick, or a hammer. The hold is always light but firm, like a relaxed fist.

Fig. 1. (above) The brush is held as vertical as possible, about two thirds of the way up the handle. The thumb and first finger oppose each other, as do the third and fourth finger. Each finger moves the brush toward one of the four cardinal points; thus the brush can be moved in a complete circle without twisting either the arm or the wrist.

Fig. 2. (center) You should be able to touch your wrist with the tip of the brush without bending your wrist.

Fig. 3. (right) Side-brushed strokes are used for painting wide bands, like bamboo, or for washes or shading.

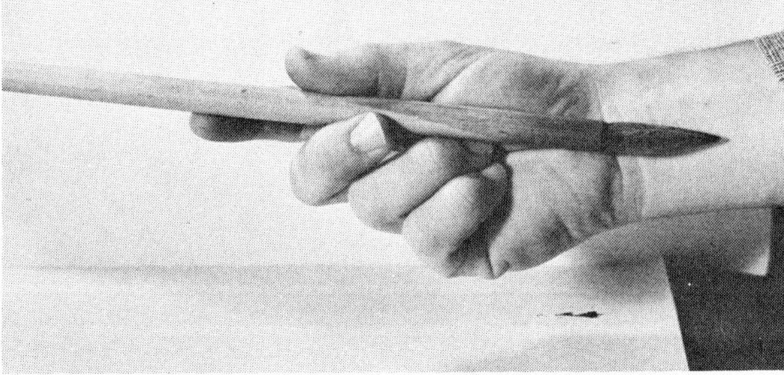

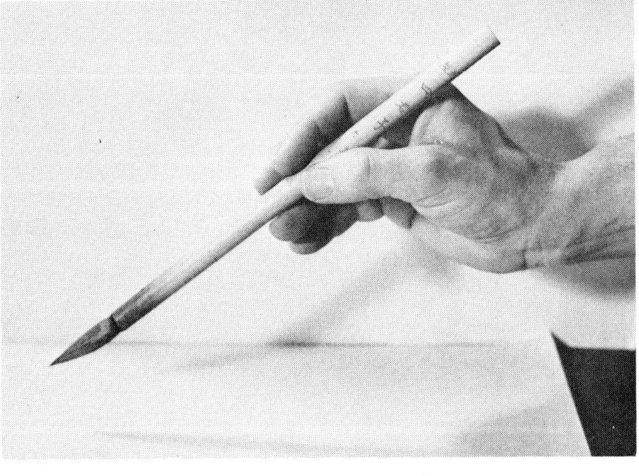

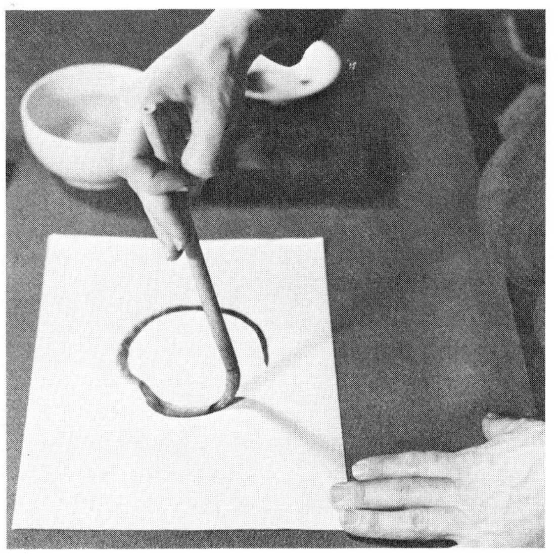 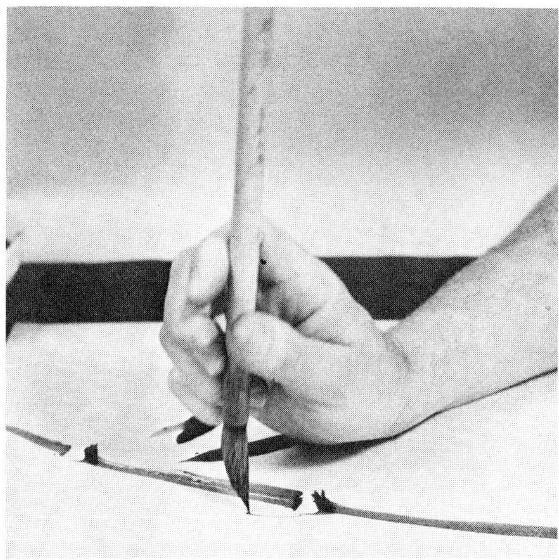

Fig. 4. (above) Most painting is done with large free movements. The wrist is kept straight, and the arm and entire body are used in the strokes.

Fig. 5. (above, right) Fine lines may be painted by grasping the brush close to the tip, so allowing the wrist to gently brush across the page. The wrist and fingers are never bent, as they are in "doodling."

Fig. 6. (below) To paint fine lines you may also use your little finger as a guide, rather than your wrist.

Moving the Brush

Brush strokes are always made with the brush tip leading the way. The brush tip is never dragged behind the brush handle. You will be using the brush correctly if you pretend it is a torch and the tip a burning fire that you must use to defend yourself from a ravenous tiger (the paper!). Remember, you must always push the tiger away from you, or he will eat you up. The proper technique for holding the brush is also similar to pushing a marble with a stick. Always push, do not pull!

Japanese brush painting is done with large free movements. Holding the brush about two thirds

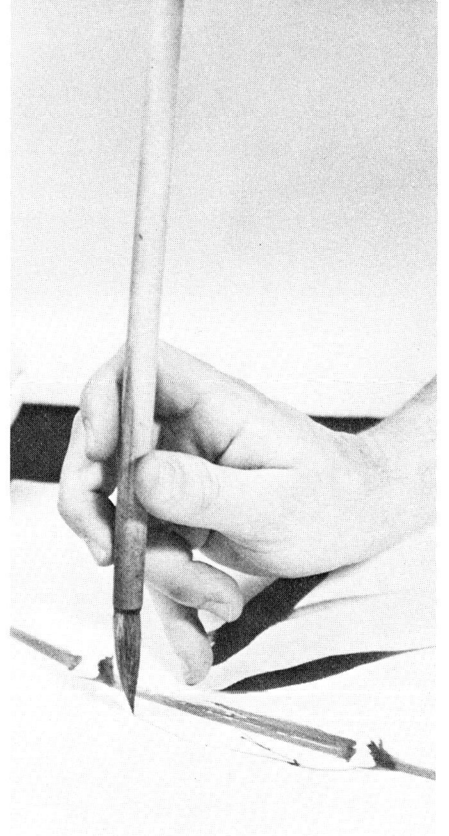

Fig. 7. Straight brush strokes are made with the tip of the brush going down the center of the stroke. This allows for variations of pressure, creating thicker and thinner lines. The stroke is fluid and graceful, expressing certainty and clearness. The brush tip leads the way.

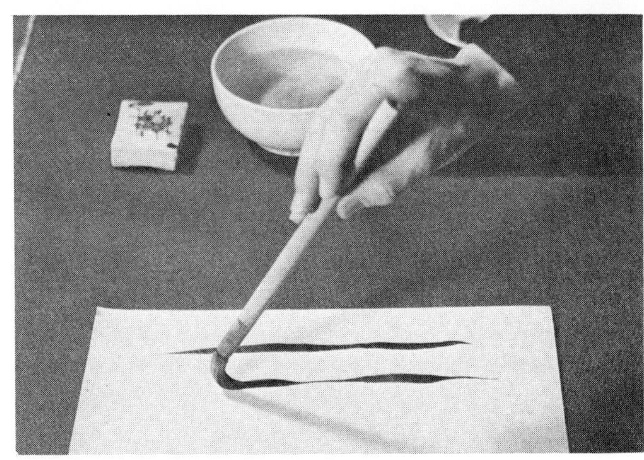

Fig. 8. Side-brushed strokes are made with the tip of the brush running along one side only of the stroke. Variations in "color" result from how much ink is used and where it is deployed on the brush tip. Thick or thin lines result from increasing or decreasing the pressure. As with straight lines, the brush tip leads the way.

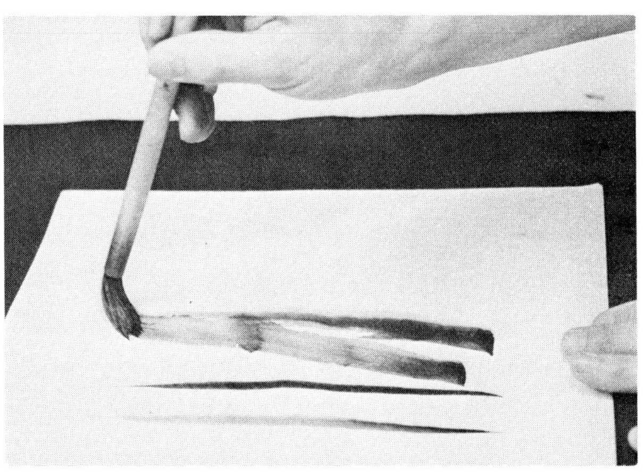

Bird.

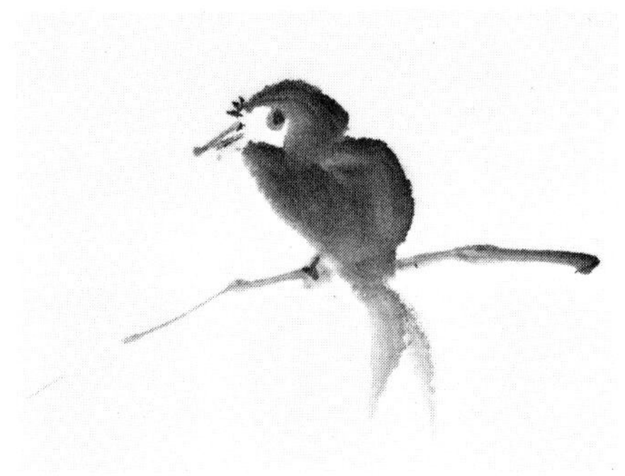

of the way up the handle, just above center, will give your brush strokes freedom and life. Holding the brush too far down the handle will produce choked, lifeless lines. Fine work, the beak of a bird, for example, is an exception. Your hand should be placed in such a way that your wrist or little finger just brushes the paper, enabling you to keep the brush vertical while painting detail work.

Types of Brush Strokes

Japanese brush painting is painterly in technique. This means subjects are filled in rather than outlined. This is called the *mokotsu* (boneless) technique, because the "bones," or outline, is not in-

58

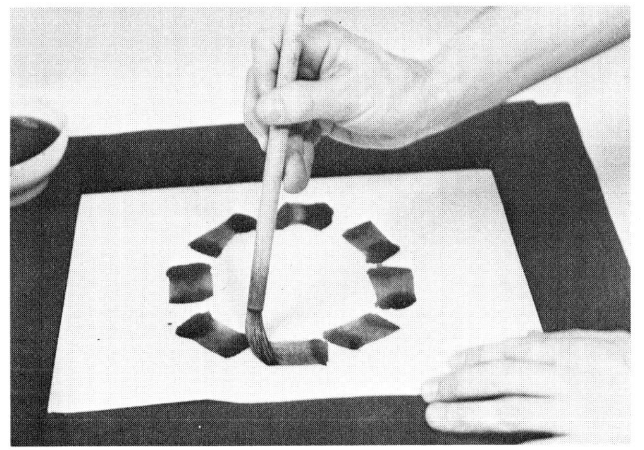

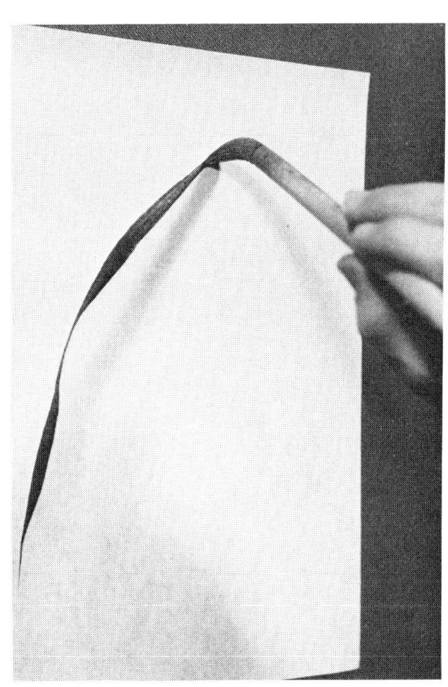

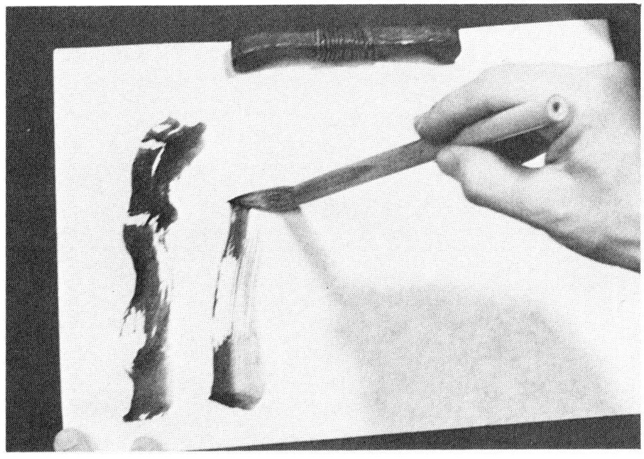

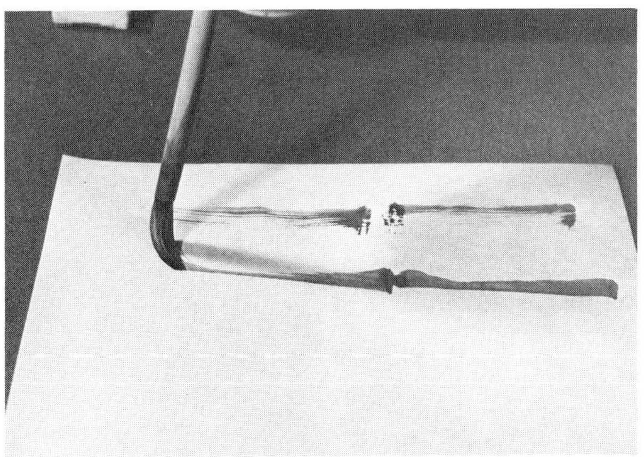

Fig. 9. (above) Straight strokes are used for outlines, detail, or, as in this case, orchid leaves. Notice the variations in pressure.

Fig. 10. (left, top) Side-brushed strokes are used for bamboo stalks and larger areas. Try brushing in all directions, moving the tip of the brush in a different direction for each stroke. The stroke opposite the one being painted was made with a downward motion, for example.

Fig. 11. (left, center) Here are two examples of the broken brush stroke. The first bole was painted with a twisted brush motion; the second demonstrates the use of a relatively dry brush.

Fig. 12. (left, bottom) The brush is painting a rapid stroke. Part of the brush lifts off the page, creating an impressionistic effect. The bamboo at top was made with a very dry brush stroke.

cluded. It is similar to Western watercolor painting in this respect.

Boneless technique requires the use of broad areas of the brush and variations in color to create an illusion of space and depth. The brush is charged with ink and manipulated in numerous ways to produce special effects of roundness or depth.

The most common strokes are the straight brush, the broad brush, and the broken brush. The straight brush stroke is strong and the brush is held as upright as is practicable for the subject. (See Fig. 9.) All the energy of concentration and purpose focuses in the point of the brush and charges the painting with life. With a brush held upright, bamboo leaves and orchid leaves reveal their strength, their stiffness, and their grace.

The broad brush stroke is made with the tip and the side of the brush. Though the brush is angled slightly, these broad strokes are painted with the intention of uprightness, but with more pressure. (See Fig. 10.) As the brush is angled further to make even broader strokes, more and more energy is deflected from the side of the stroke painted by the point. Care must be taken neither to let the brush angle become too great, nor to lose the sense of pushing the brush.

The broken brush technique, or broken ink technique, refers to a variety of techniques and styles,

Broad Strokes and Three-Ink Technique. Painting with multiple shading is done with the three-ink technique. Some of its uses are illustrated. The broad stroke, which uses the side of the brush to create a wider line, is particularly suitable to this technique.

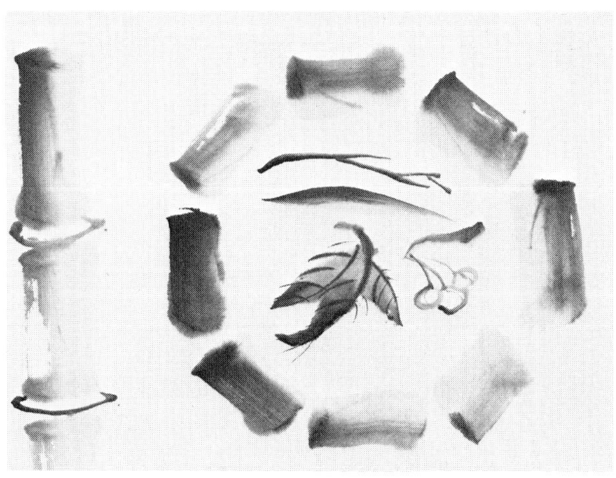

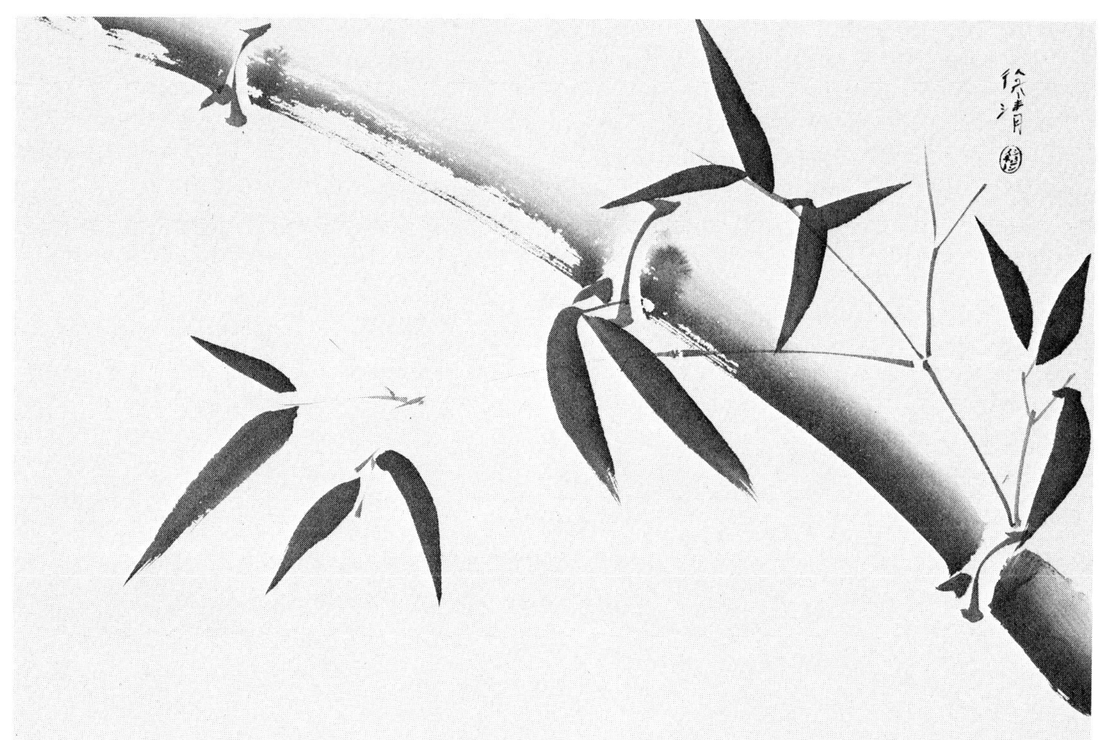

which depend for their effect upon interrupting
the flow of ink onto the page. This can be done
in three ways: (1) by using a "dry brush," a brush
that has little water in it, to create a streaked texture (Fig. 11, at right); (2) by moving the brush
in an uneven way, frequently changing direction,
varying the pressure, and twisting it so as to create
a spontaneous and impressionistic effect (Fig. 11,
at left); (3) by moving the brush so quickly that
parts of the brush are deflected from the paper or
fail to touch it, creating a free and open effect
(Fig. 12).

Space. What is unsaid, the emptiness of the paper, contributes as
much to the painting as does the
quality of the bamboo stalk.

Understatement: The White Space

My students often want to know the difference
between Japanese and Chinese painting. I tell
them that the Japanese paint a scene with one
less leaf. The spirit of sumi-e is what distinguish-
es it from Chinese painting. Sumi-e is the art of
the unsaid, of the unpainted.

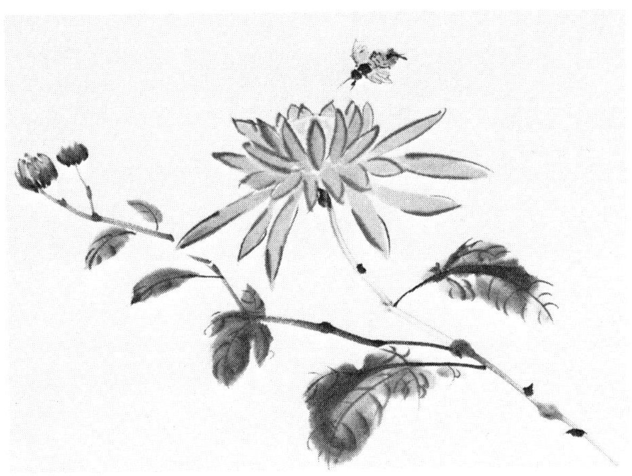

Early Chrysanthemum. Notice the variety of colors employed and the effect of shading in the leaves. The petals were outlined to highlight them. The outline was added after the petal was painted, but before the ink was completely dry.

The effect of sumi-e depends on the composition, and on the interplay of black, white, and grey. Subjects are whittled to simplicity: a part of a branch rather than the whole tree; a bamboo shooting off the edge of the painting; two birds representing the universe. The feelings and intention of the painter are embodied in the use of color and the brushwork. But most important is what is not painted, the tension between two or three forms in a white space, the very whiteness giving birth to the meaning of the brush strokes.

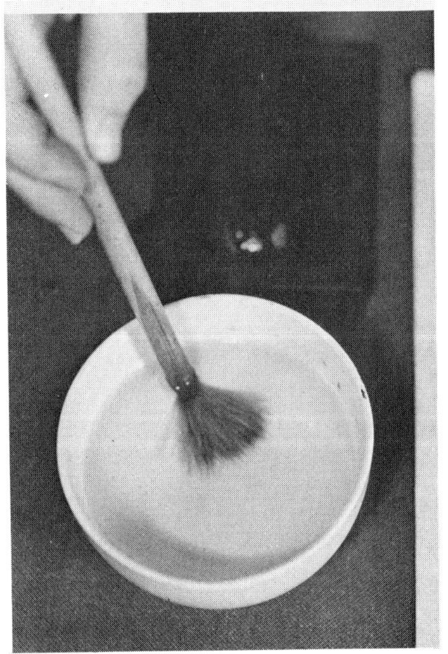

Fig. 13. The brush is wetted thoroughly in relatively "white" water.

The Colors of Sumi-e

Black and white painting is a special way of seeing the world, like black and white photography or movies. Black, white, and the various shades of grey create a range of colors as varied as any palette, even though the "colors" of sumi-e are not colors in the usual sense.

An old tradition tells us there are five "colors" in sumi-e. Black, which we normally consider colorless, and its opposite, white, which actually contains all the colors, are two of the five. The color between black and white, medium grey, is another. The last two are the grey between black and medium grey, and the grey between white and medium grey. An examination of almost any sumi-e painting will reveal, however, that there is actually a much greater variety of grey tones than these five.

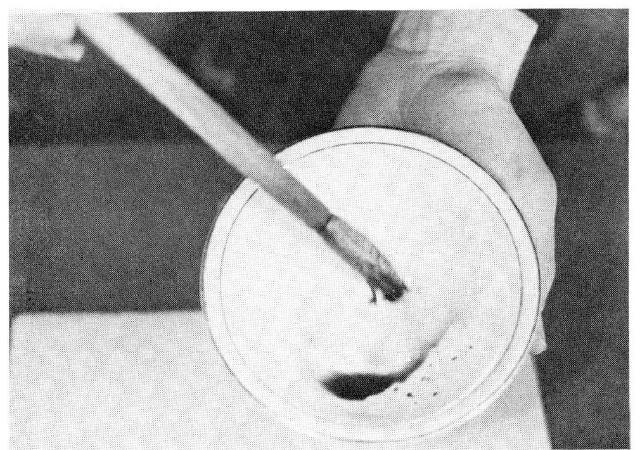

Fig. 14. Taking a small amount of ink from the ink stone onto the tip of the brush, a medium grey color is created.

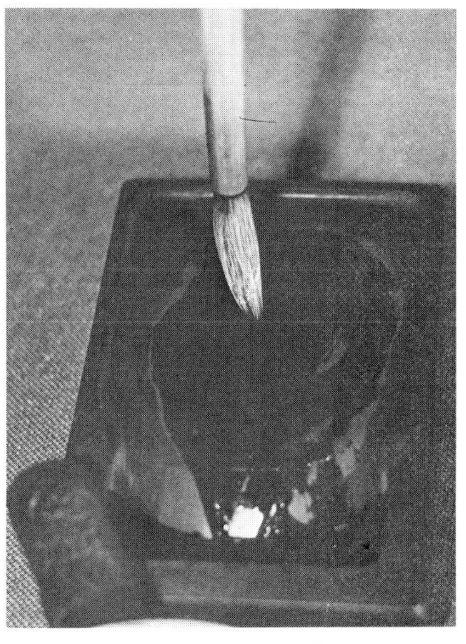

Fig. 15. With grey color covering half the brush, the tip only is touched to the ink stone to add a dark color.

Fig. 16. A side-brushed stroke will produce a line in which a variety of tones will blend into each other to create a rounded effect.

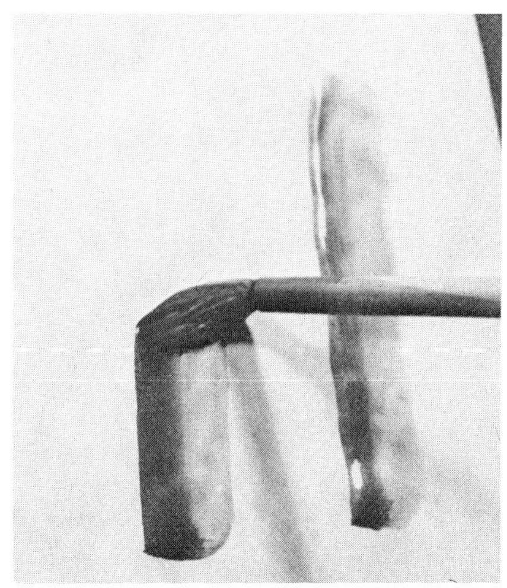

Three-Ink Technique

Color effects are heightened in sumi-e by the use of multiple ink shading techniques. Some of these are similar to traditional watercolor techniques. Dark ink can be added to a light wash, causing the dark ink to run. Or light washes can be added to dark areas to create a two-toned effect. Another common method of shading found in sumi-e is the three-ink technique. Three colors of ink are put on one brush — white, grey, and black. The brush is first dipped in the wash water (white); then it is dipped into a medium grey color, about half-way up the bristles, and finally the tip is dipped into the darkest ink on the ink stone. If a relatively wet brush is used, the three colors run into each other on the paper, producing a multi-toned effect. If the brush is too wet, however, or if too much black ink is taken onto the tip, the ink will "run" too quickly and the entire stroke will turn black. If too little water is used, the three "colors" will not blend. The separation of colors in one stroke will add instead a stiff angularity to the painting. Care must be taken to use neither too much water nor too much ink. Practicing this technique with varying degrees of wetness and different tones of grey will soon give you control over the effects it can create.

Chapter 6

TECHNIQUE: THE TAIL OF THE TIGER

Techniques are the tools of artistic creation and pleasure. To ride the tiger — as the Eastern myth has it — one must first catch it by the tail. Acquiring the skills of painting allows us to determine our own path and venture into new realms.

Technique is an umbrella for a variety of skills: control of the brush, the amount of water in the brush, color determination, spatial relationships, proportion, fidelity to the subject being painted, and the multitude of procedures, subtleties, and recipes involved in learning to paint almost any subject. The essential fact about the skills we label technique is that they are all learned through practice and experiment.

The Bite.   Another example of combining painting and inscription. In this case the reference is to the common expression after a drinking binge, "I have to get a hair of the dog that bit me." Notice the use of the dry-brush technique in the robe. This painting was almost wholly outline in technique.

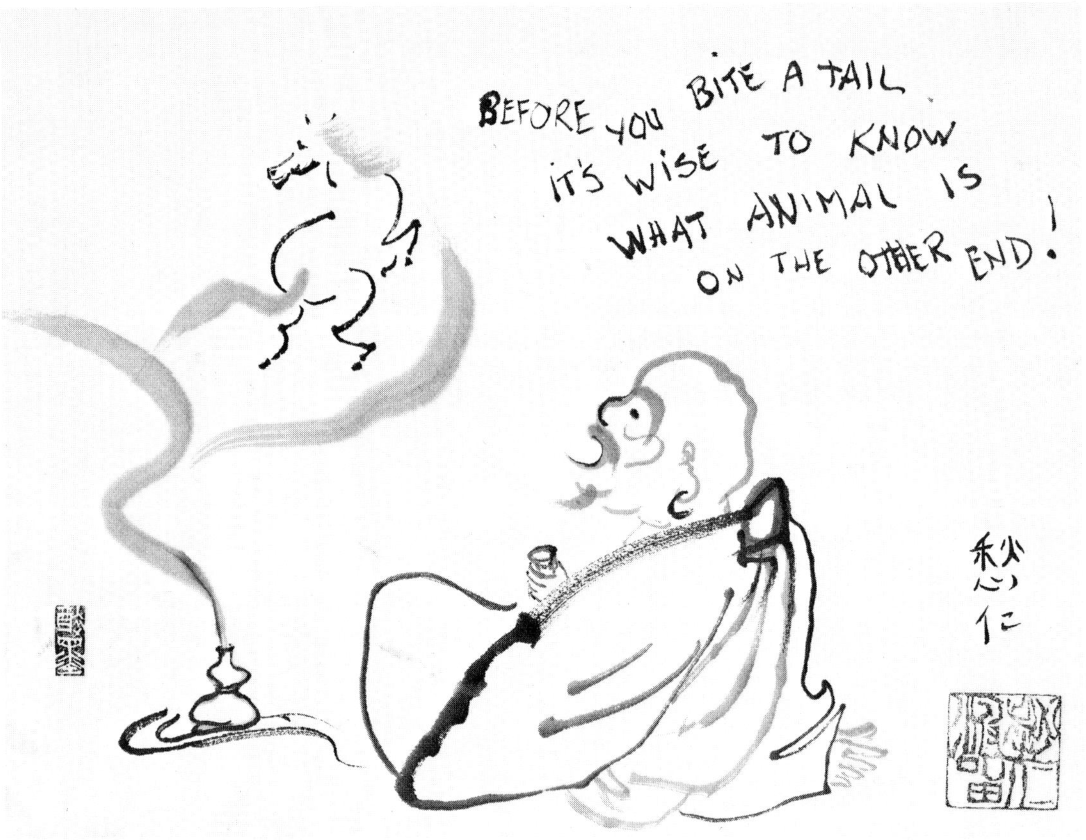

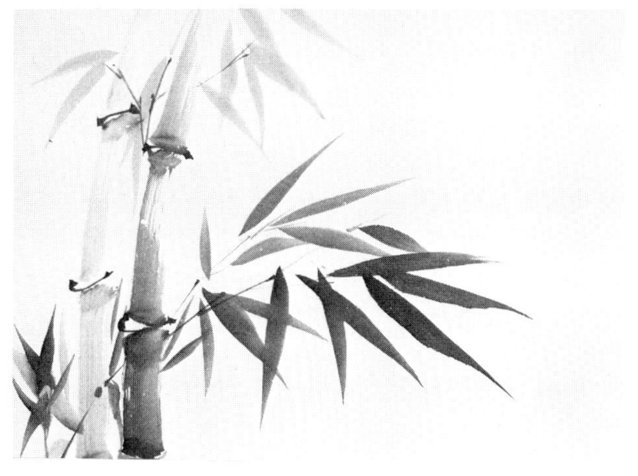

Spring Morning.

Two of the traditional subjects of sumi-e are bamboo and orchids. They are usually the first subjects taught, because of the variety of techniques required. They are also, for the same reason, the last mastered. There is much to learn from painting them, for they are a continual wellspring of inspiration. Painting them gives you a solid grounding in sumi-e because they contain the important strokes and techniques for everything else you will paint. They introduce the major elements of sumi-e composition — spacing, depth, color, gradation, perspective — all the various elements that go into creating a painting, including rhythm and focus. But most important these compositions will give you a sense of the spirit with which sumi-e painting is approached.

Bamboo

Bamboo is the emblematic image of the Orient. Having an almost limitless variety of uses, bamboo has been a favorite subject of painters for centuries. Its perfect combination of strength and grace makes it beautiful the year round, whether bent by storm and rain, swayed by summer's gentle breezes, enshrouded in spring's delicate mist, or silhouetted by a fine layer of snow.

The beauty and strength of bamboo, long a symbol of perseverance and fidelity, are at the core

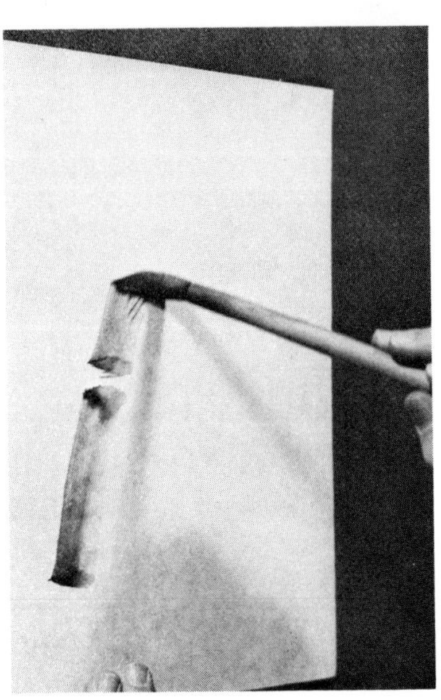

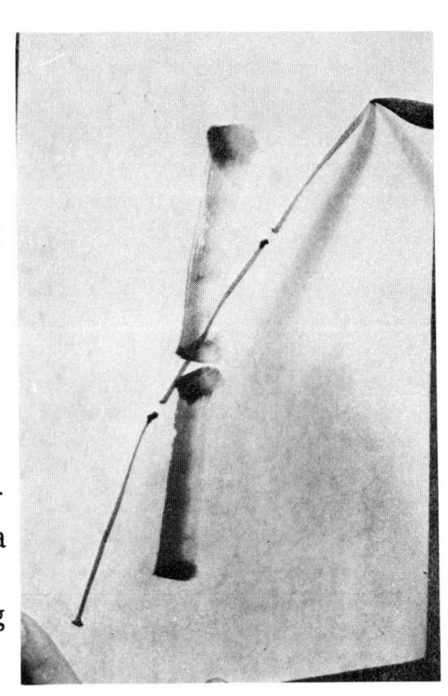

Fig. 17. Bamboo boles are painted by moving the brush from joint to joint in a steady rhythm. Each stalk has a unity of execution which can be enhanced by painting an entire stalk in a single exhalation of breath.

Fig. 18. Thin stalks and branches have the exact same construction as their larger prototypes. Using a dry brush will prevent the thin stems from becoming too thick.

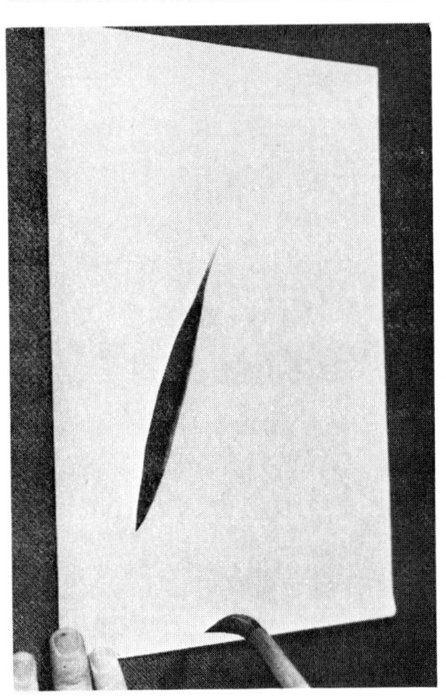

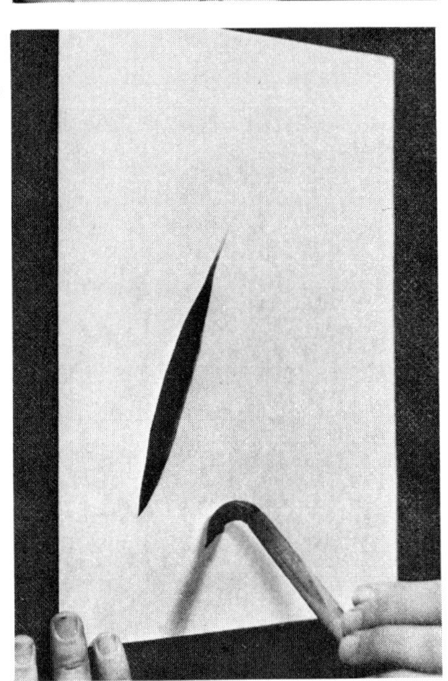

Fig. 19. Bamboo leaves begin and end far off the page. Like an airplane landing and taking off, we see only the traces of the time on the ground, but there is a long flight path before and after the brush touches paper. Here the brush approaches the paper.

Fig. 20. The beginning of a leaf. Note that the brush tip leads the way.

Fig. 21. The earlier part of the leaf is fuller and must be painted with more pressure.

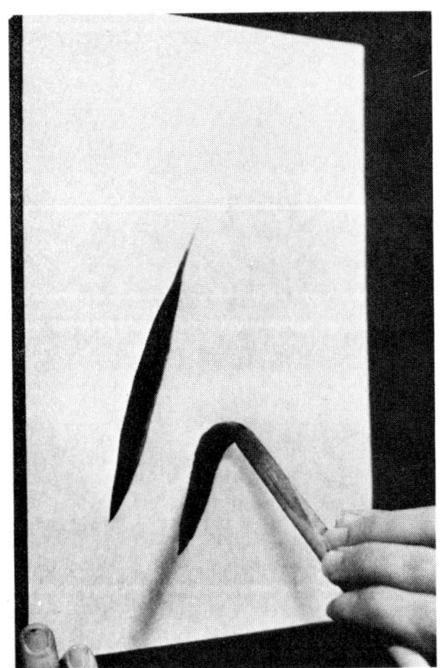

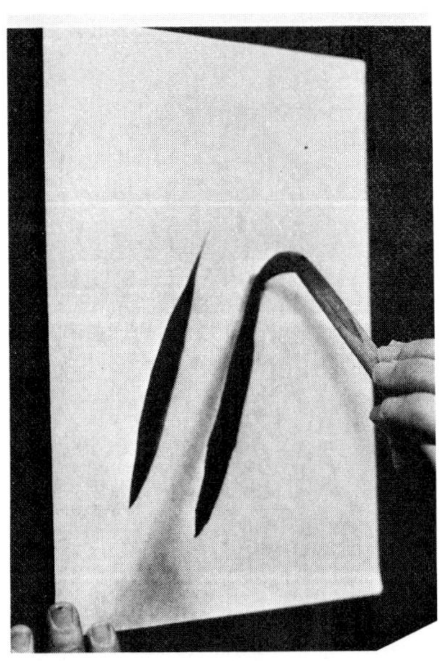

Fig. 22. The leaf gradually becomes thinner as pressure is released.

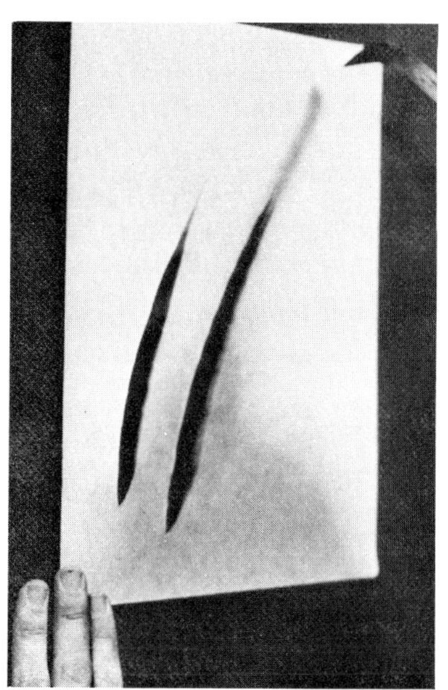

Fig. 23. The leaf is completed, but the brush keeps moving.

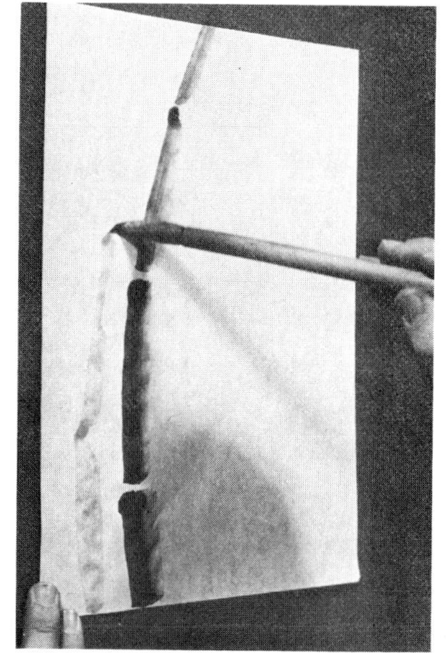

Fig. 24. The stalks are usually painted first. Note the different colors of each stalk, which create distance, and the different levels of the joints, which create more interest.

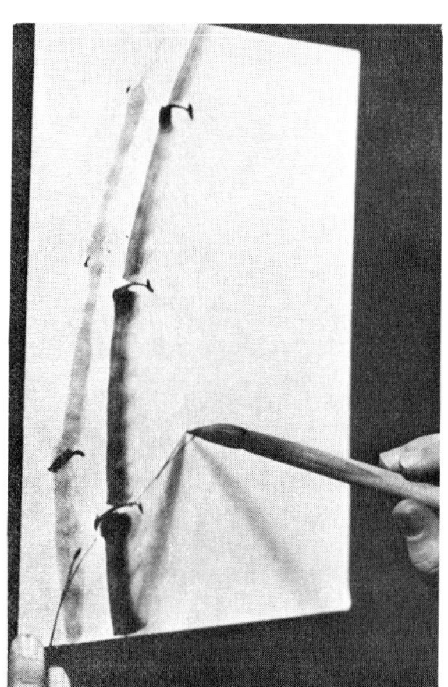

Fig. 25. The thin stems are added next. It is only necessary to make a rough frame to hang the leaves on.

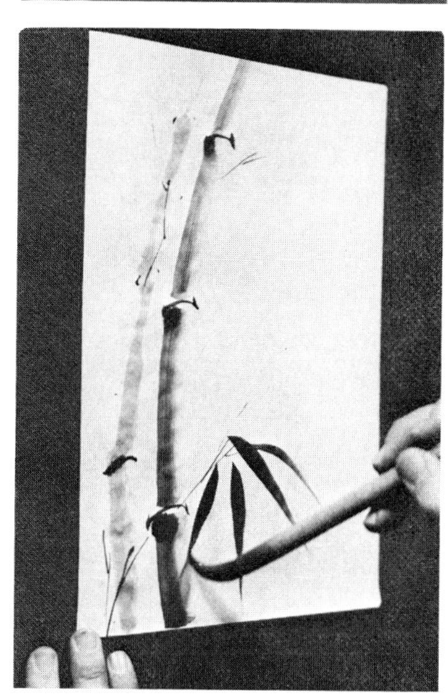

Fig. 26. The large, major dark leaves are painted first.

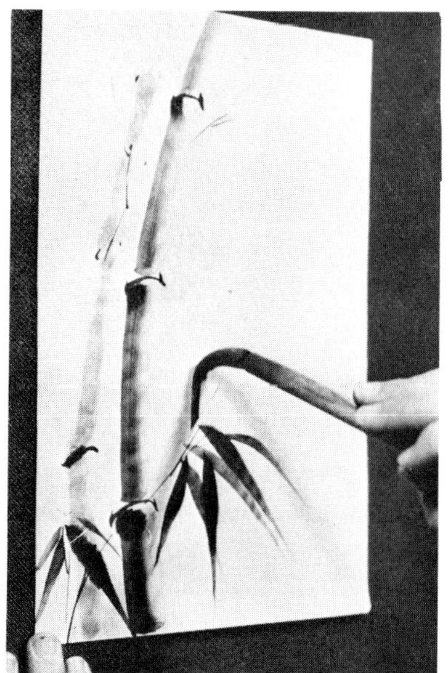

Fig. 27. The lighter, medium-colored leaves forming the second level are painted.

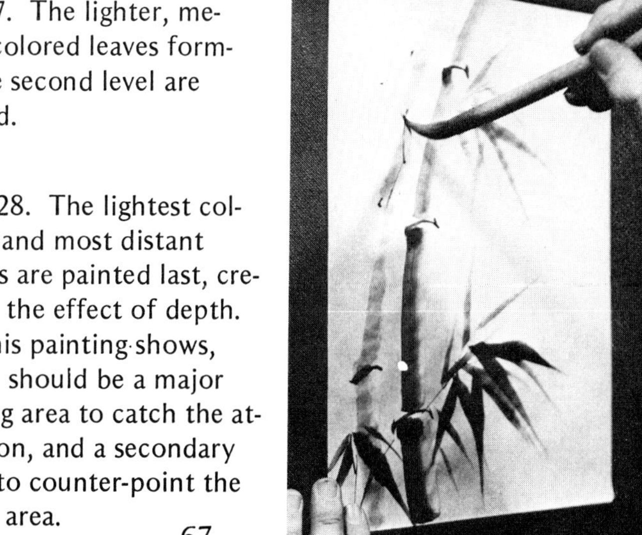

Fig. 28. The lightest colored and most distant leaves are painted last, creating the effect of depth. As this painting shows, there should be a major strong area to catch the attention, and a secondary area to counter-point the main area.

of its being. Starting in the spring from young
bamboo shoots, the plant literally "shoots" into
the air, achieving 90 per cent of its fifty to eighty
foot maturity in one month, and completing its
growth within another thirty days. It sprouts so
fast that researchers report being able to actually
see it grow.

To paint bamboo properly our brush must capture this incredible spirit, strength, and grace.
We must feel its growth, how it sways in the wind
without breaking, how it endures extremes of
temperature without dying. Like pine, it is green
year round, yet in its gracefulness how unlike
pine! Each stalk of bamboo should be painted
in a single long breath; so, too, each cluster of
leaves.

Bamboo is the most difficult of all sumi-e subjects to master. In its combination of delicacy
and strength, however, lies the key to all the rest
of sumi-e. The painting, "Spring Morning," is
made up of several parts, each requiring unique
handling of the brush. The stalks are strong and
broad, the stems are delicate yet stiff, the leaves
firm yet very smooth. The strokes that make up
bamboo will be found in many other paintings.

The making of stalk and stem is illustrated in
"Stalks and Joints of Bamboo," on page 69. Stalk
1 is a uniform light color since bamboo stalks are
usually lighter in color, yellow in contrast to the
green of the leaves. Stalk 2 shows the use of the
three-ink technique, as does Fig. 16 and the painting on page 60. Stalk 3 is darker and in its brevity
gives a feeling of wetness, as does much of the
dry-brush technique (see "Space," on page 61,
for example). Stalks 4 and 5 are thinner examples.
And Stalk 6 shows the placement of the stems.
(Notice that they alternate sides.)

Bamboo is not painted, but rather strung between joints. The brush is placed sideways, though
roughly vertical, as shown in the photograph.
Resting the brush at joint *a,* the bole is formed by
moving the brush quickly to *b.* Do not try to
paint the bole. Simply move the brush from rest

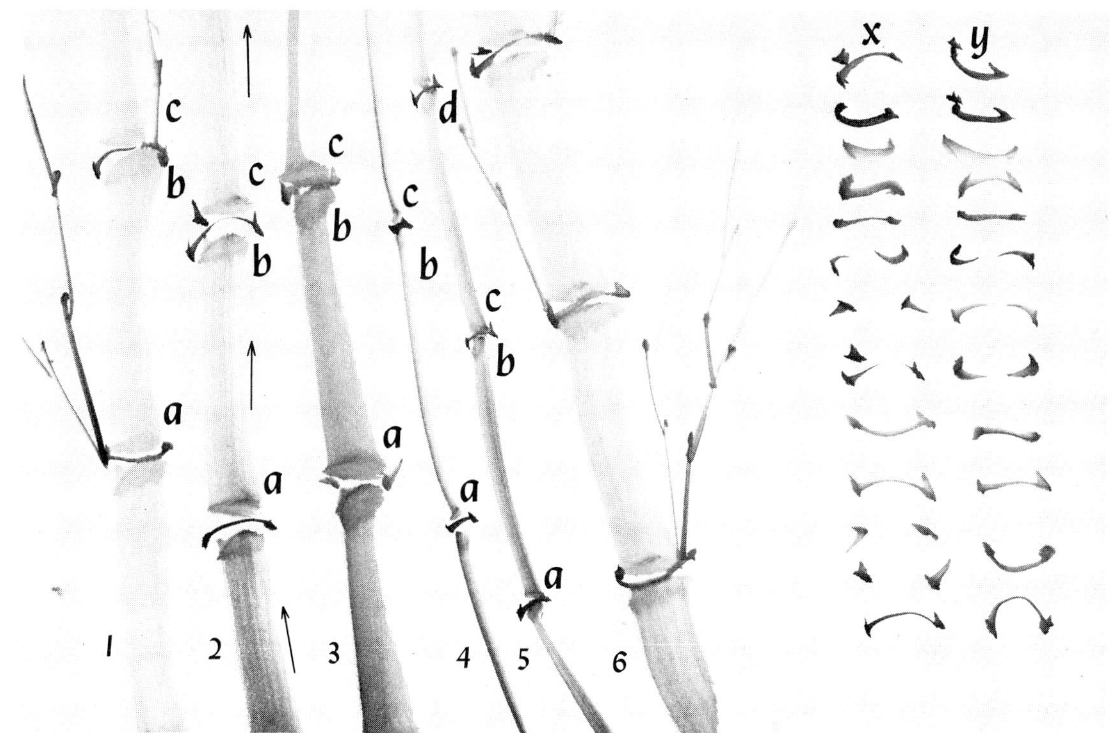

at *a* to rest at *b* as quickly as is appropriate to the energy you want to express in your bamboo. Then lift the brush slightly, place it down again at joint *c*, move it quickly to the next joint, rest a second and lift again. The sections between joints are not painted, they simply materialize when you spurt from the bottom joint to the top joint.

Stalks are made by pushing the brush away from you, not by dragging the brush. You should be able to look right down the brush, like pushing a broom. Rather than trying to see what you're painting, focus on what it is like to be bamboo springing into the air, section by section. Boles are very stiff and straight, yet the bamboo stalk has an overall inclination to the ground. Do not make stalks straight as an arrow. Slant each section of a stalk in a slightly different direction from the sections above and below it, and also give each stalk a different tilt from the stalks to either side.

The joints are painted in with a relatively dry brush, often slightly darker than the bamboo bole itself. Several types of joints are illustrated, though there are others. When painting the joints, keep

Stalks and Joints of Bamboo.
Bamboo stalks are painted in a variety of widths and lengths, though the brush is held in essentially the same manner for all. As the arrows accompanying Stalk 2 point out, each section of the stalk has a slightly different inclination. Notice that the small branches are painted the same way as stalks, straight and stiff. They will bend only at the very end, from the weight of the leaves.

perspective in mind. Joints will be like the top
joint in column *y* if they are below eye level, like
the bottom joint in column *x* if above eye level,
and rather horizontal if at eye level. Stalk 6 illustrates the three main types.

"Stalk Skeleton," below, shows the skeleton of
bamboo. Compare it to "Spring Morning," on
page 65. When making bamboo, make each section slightly longer than the last, as bamboo grows
that way, the sections near the ground being
short, the middle sections getting longer, until
near the top the sections get shorter again. When
making two stalks, your picture will be most interesting if you make one smaller than the other,
and if you make one darker. Do not place the
joints in the same places, either. The smaller
branches, or stems, are made with a very dry brush,
though their structure is the same as their parent
trunks. Make them the same way you make the
trunks, going from joint to joint, rather than painting in the section between the joints.

"Making Leaves," on page 71, shows the many
ways to make bamboo leaves. Leaves are bilateral, with two identical halves and a vein down the
middle. When painting them, however, we either
paint them face on (leaf *c* in each corner and the
four top leaves) or with the vein on top or bottom (*a* and *b* show the vein on top, and *d* and *e*

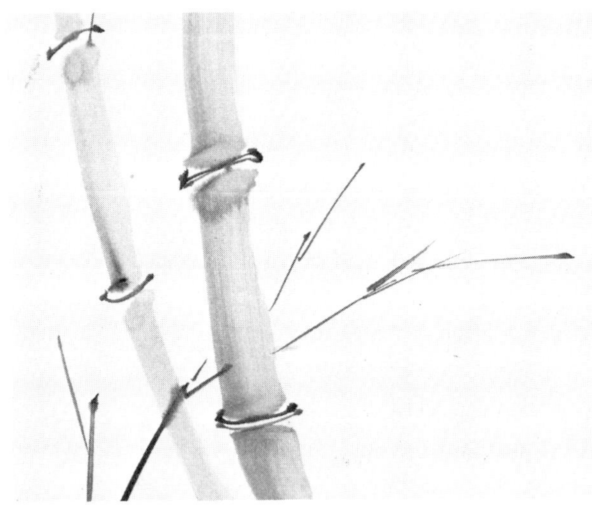

Stalk Skeleton. Only a few basic
stems are put in before the leaves
are painted. After the leaves are
placed, connecting stems are added.

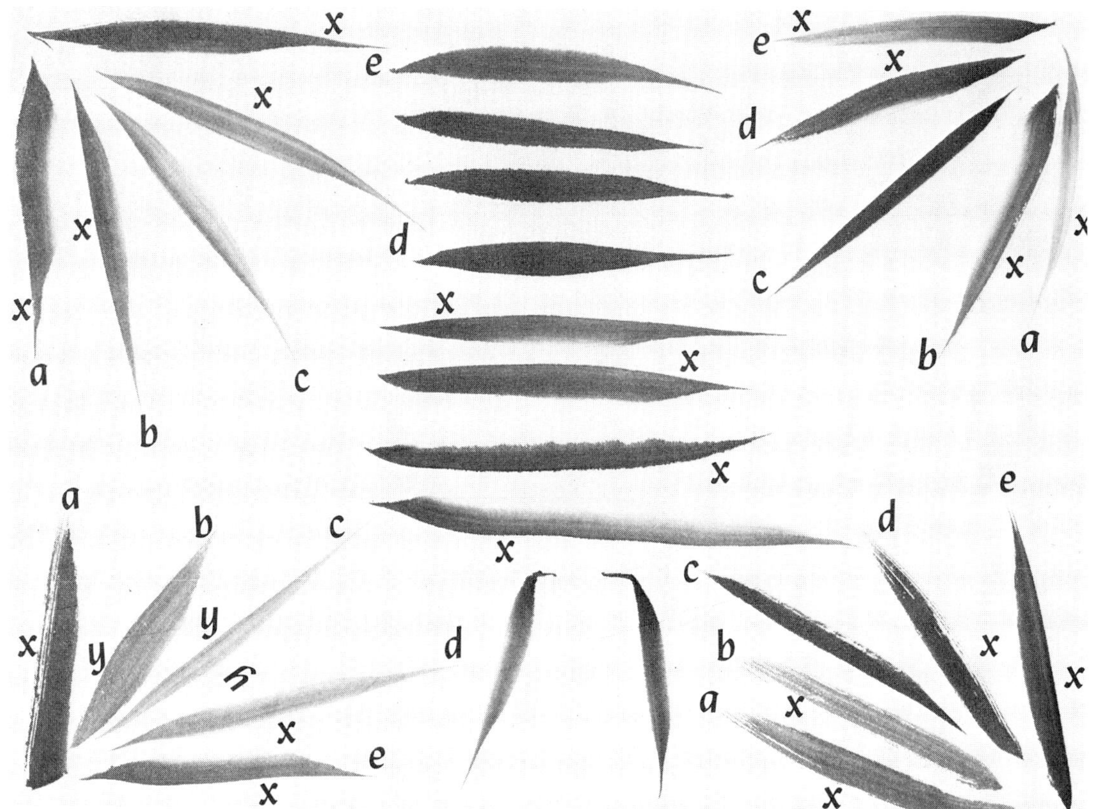

show it on the bottom). The vein, which runs down the center of the leaf and gives it support, is always straighter than the uneven edge of the leaf. Side x is the vein, and the other side is the outer edge.

When painting leaves, face-on leaves are produced by holding the brush straight so the tip of the brush goes down the center of the leaf. As with the stalk, you must push away from you slightly, as if pushing a marble with the tip of your index finger. Moving the brush slightly right or left of vertical will produce side views of the leaves. The tip of the brush produces the vein, x, and the middle of the brush produces the rough edge, y. Try to keep your wrist straight, as the leaves are painted with the entire body, and especially the forearm.

A good exercise for leaf painting is to complete a circle, like the leaves in the four corners of "Mak-

Making Leaves. Bamboo leaves grow in all four directions, so it is good to practice drawing them in all possible ways. The leaves in the top corners were painted with a relatively wet brush, those in the bottom corners with a drier brush. The leaves in the center give some examples of leaf shapes. The bottom leaf is a good example of the use of three-ink technique to paint a leaf.

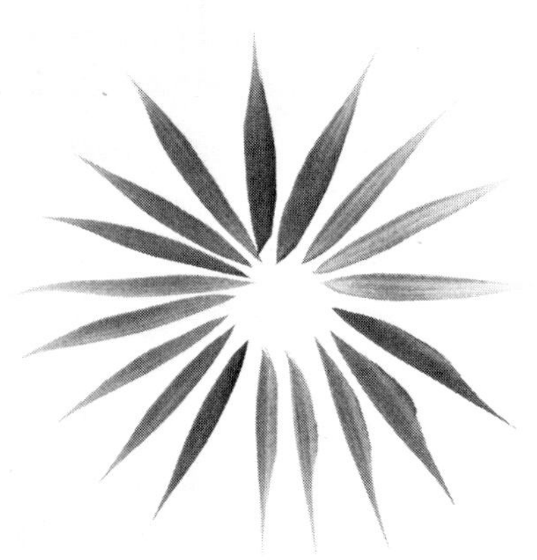

Leaf Circle.   The leaf stroke is a basic stroke in sumi-e and requires many skills — precision, grace, rhythm, and delicacy. Most important of all, however, is free movement of the entire arm.

ing Leaves," page 71, or the leaves in "Leaf Circle," at left.

"Leaf Patterns," below, shows the various combinations of leaves. These should be practiced (as well as others you discover yourself). In any one grouping, leaves are never of the same size; they usually have different shapes and point in different directions. In any one cluster, groups of leaves will often be painted from a single brush-load of ink and will therefore be of approximately the same color. As you can see, it is best that the leaves do not emanate from the same point, and that not all of them touch.

When you are ready, try combining all these elements into one painting, either by devising one yourself or by copying one from this book or elsewhere. Copying is one of the best ways to learn composition skills; do not hesitate to imitate other paintings. Soon you will be creating your own!

Japanese Orchids

Like bamboo, orchid is one of the classical sumi-e subjects, noteworthy for its combination of graceful leaves and delicate multihued flowers. The strokes that go into its composition are used in many paintings. More so than bamboo, the white space that is set off by the arching leaves determines the over-all tone and mood of the compo-

Leaf Patterns. Leaves are painted rather intuitively, but some basic patterns are commonly accepted as characteristic of bamboo. These several patterns are often used in combination when more leaves are required or when depth is needed.

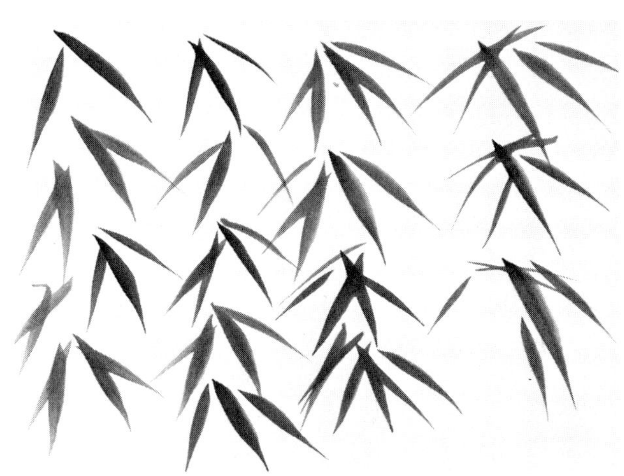

sition. Though orchids seem to fill the page, there are often only two or three leaves and flowers.

"Orchids," at right, consists mainly of leaves and flowers. The types of leaves are illustrated in "Orchid Leaves," page 76. As in bamboo, three types of leaves are made: straight leaves, *a*, and two types of side-brushed leaves, *b* and *c*. Type *d* is a combination of straight and side stroke. Leaves *d* and *e* illustrate using the brush in two different directions. Leaf *f* simply turns back on itself before becoming side brushed.

Straight leaves are illustrated in "Straight Leaves," page 76. Leaf *a* is a straight leaf made with the point of the brush going down the center, as you can see if you look carefully at the dark line in the center of the leaf. Leaves *b* and *c* are made with the same brush charge of ink. Notice that the lighter leaves seem further away, as if painted on a wetter day. Leaves *d* and *e* are painted with one side of the brush only charged with ink. Leaves *f*, *g*, *h*, and *i* have both sides charged but not the center. The small leaves at the bottom illustrate how to make the shorter leaves near the base of the plant.

Side-brushed orchid leaves are shown on page 77. Leaf *a* is wide and *b* is very thin. Leaves *c* through *g* were made with one charge of ink on one side only of the brush. Leaves *h*, *i*, *j*, and *k* are charged on two sides of the brush and show rougher, wetter-looking forms. Leaves *l*, *m*, and *n* show various smaller versions of combination straight- and side-brushed leaves.

Orchid leaves are made like bamboo leaves, in that you must push away with the brush, rather than letting it trail along behind your hand. Leaves are somewhat stiff, except for a gentle bend in them and a final heavenward turning at the end.

The flowers of the orchid plant are illustrated on page 78. When painting flowers, start with a clean, relatively dry brush, touching only the very tip into black ink. This will produce petals which at the tips are dark and which shade into grey toward the center. You may have to renew

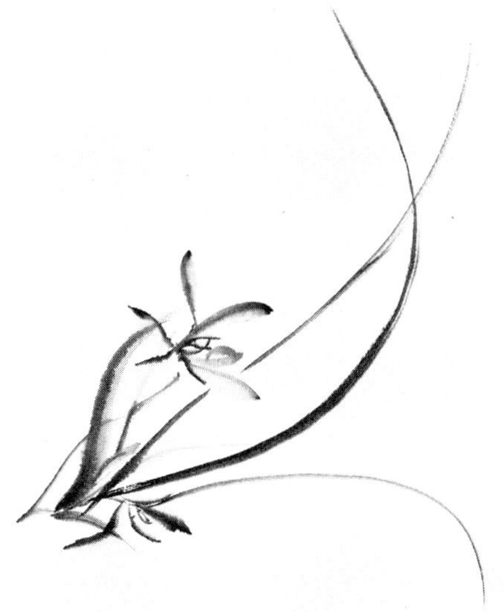

Orchids.

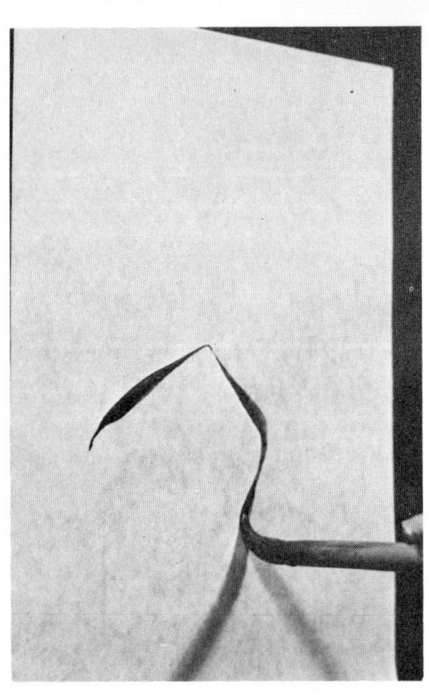

Fig. 29. The most important leaf is painted first, often in a dark color. Note the variations in pressure and direction.

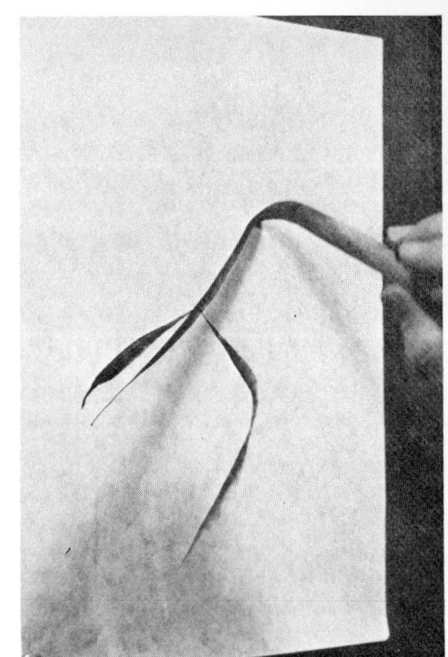

Fig. 30. Next paint the secondary leaves. Only three or four leaves are necessary.

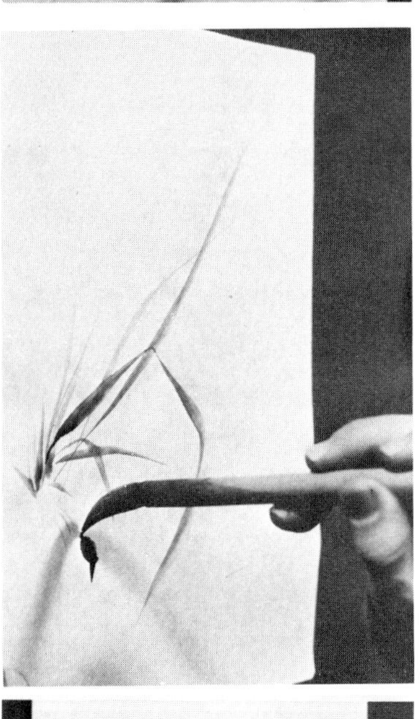

Fig. 31. Flowers are painted from the inside out, beginning here with the two smallest petals overlapping each other.

Fig. 32. The third petal is larger and shows a delicate blush of color. The brush is first rinsed in clear water, then the tip only is touched to the black ink of the ink stone. This produces petals which are dark at the tip and fade into the most delicate grey.

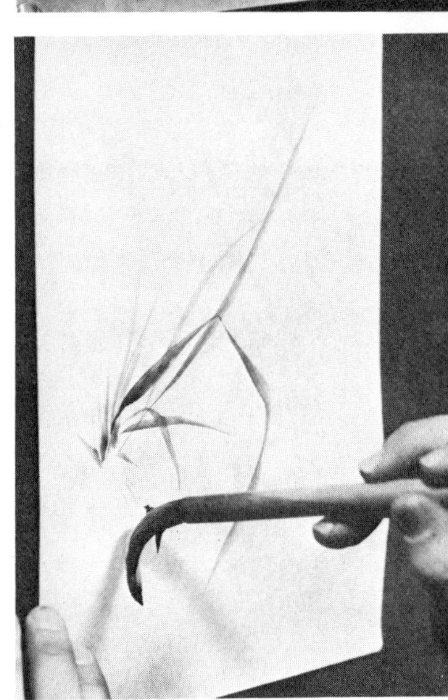

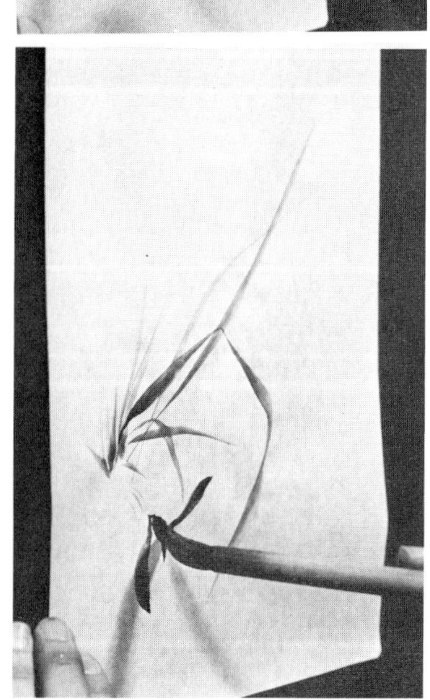

Fig. 33. The fourth petal is added. It should be a different size and be attached at a different angle from the third petal. The same is true of the fifth petal. Finally, three small dots are added to represent the innards of the flower.

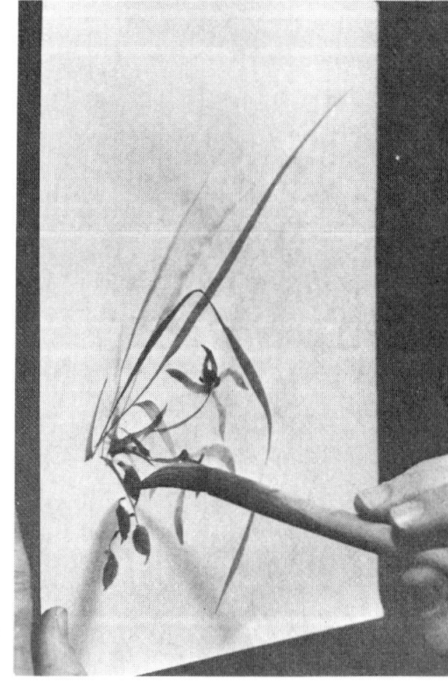

Fig. 34. Unopened buds are painted like two overlapping petals.

the black tip, as it gets used up after one or two
petals. Not immediately, but before the petals
dry, add the three dots representing the flower's
internal parts. Stems and new, unopened flowers are drawn as shown.

Pointers on Composition

Sumi-e is a spare language in which the white
space often speaks in eloquent conversation with
the tones of black and grey. The clear and rapid
placement of the few strokes and forms is critical to a painting's over-all effect. Thus, a mono-
tone tree placed in the center of the paper is
less attractive and interesting than a multihued
one off to the side which allows a view past it to
two or three small lightly shaded trees in the distance. Too many trees will muddy the painting,
however, destroying the simple counterpoint of
two or three.

The following suggestions can be applied as
general guidelines to composition.

1. Foreground is painted first, background
later.

2. Primary subject is painted first, secondary
next, and tertiary last. Many paintings are ar-
ranged in this way. This is called variously *Ten
Chi Jin* (heaven, earth, man) or *Shukakuju* (host,
guest, servant), essentially referring to a three-
part composition. The eye should be attracted

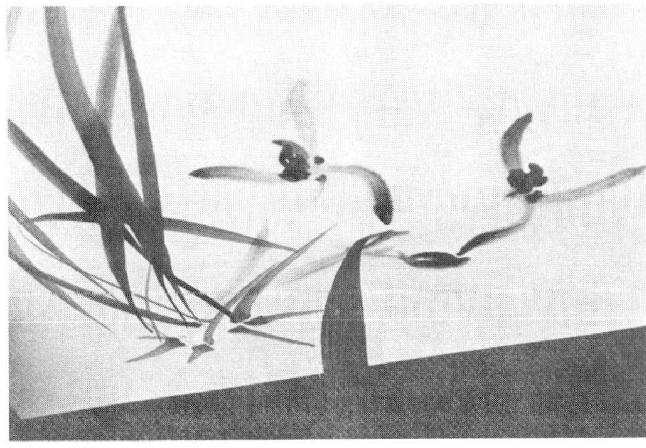

Fig. 35. Notice the shading of the
petals, the placement of the three
dots, and the construction of the
buds.

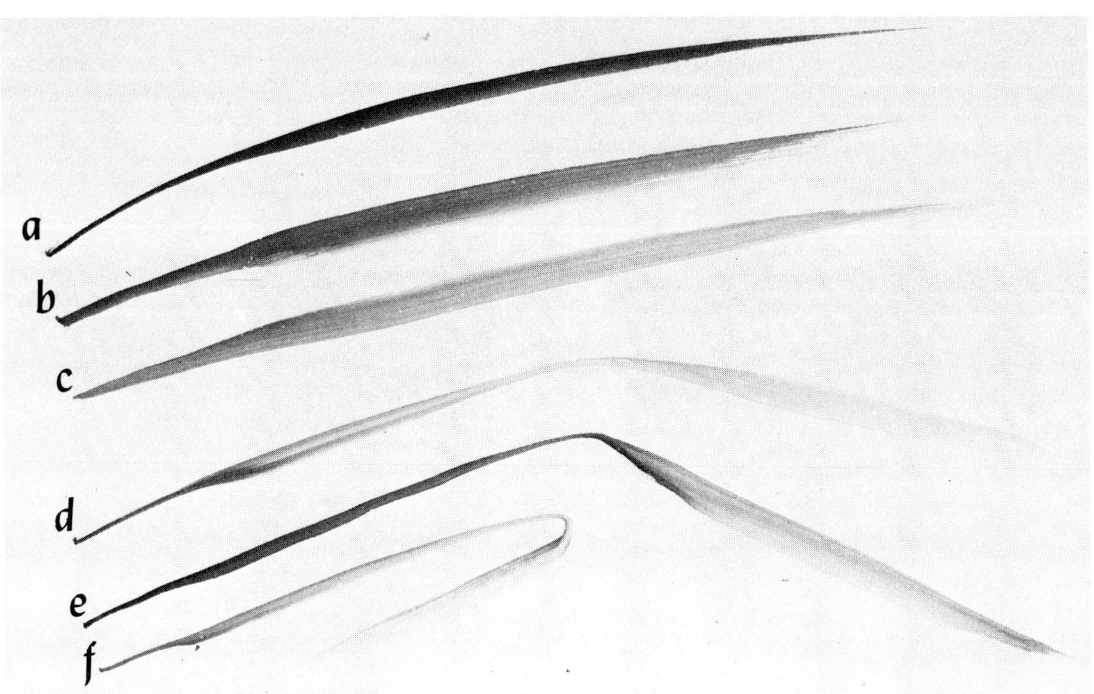

Orchid Leaves. Note that the bottom three leaves require two different brush positions. The brush is turned without stopping, requiring a very subtle transition to avoid any wavering in the line.

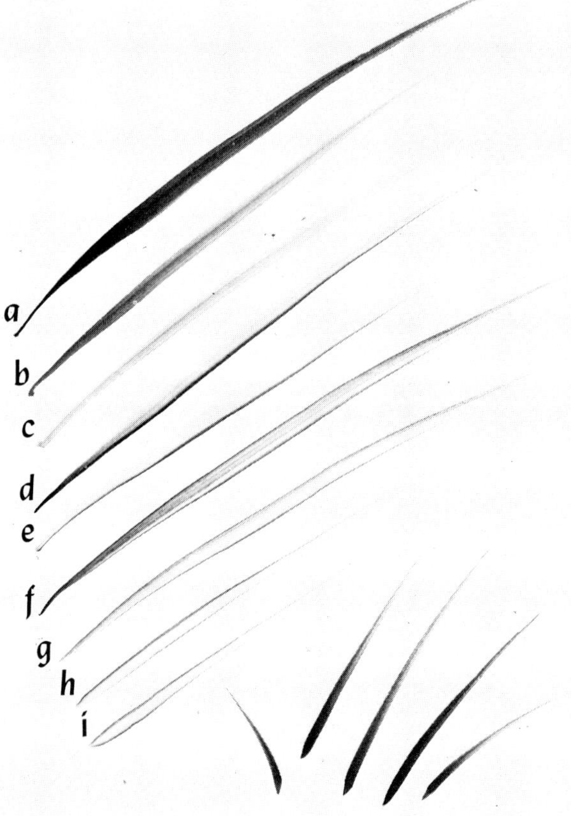

Straight Leaves. Notice that while there is a gentle curve to the leaf, the final portion approaching the tip is painted with the intention of "reaching toward heaven." Simply keeping in mind your intention that the tip have a slight upward leaning at the end will usually be enough to produce this essential requirement of good orchid leaves.

to the most important area first, then the second,
then the third, and finally back to the first,
flowing thus in a rough unity. From this rule
comes the next.

  3. Darkest areas are painted first, then lighter.
Thus dark bamboo leaves are painted first, the
lighter ones over this, creating the effect of depth.
If lighter leaves are painted first, then the wetness
of the paper would cause the dark ink to run into
the lighter leaves. The opposite does not happen,
because the light ink has no effect on the dark
ink (unless there is too much water).

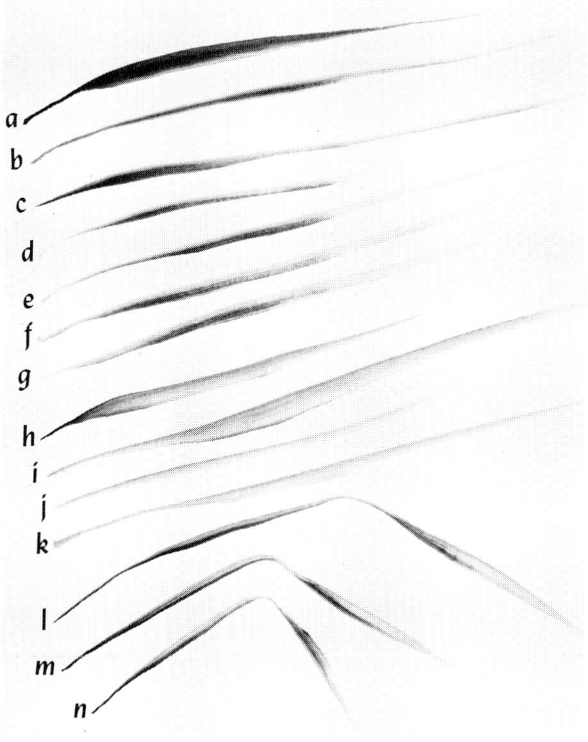

Side-Brushed Orchid Leaves.
Notice the use of the three-ink
technique.

  4. Facial details are done first when painting
animals, birds, and people. This is because proportion depends largely on the head and face, and
also because the rest of the body will follow the
personality or feeling of the face.

  5. Use one brush for an entire composition.
This gives a feeling of unity to the brush work.

It also helps you develop skill in the handling of your brush. Occasionally, a small brush is used for detail work, or an outline brush is used to paint fine outlines. Separate brushes are often used to add colors as well.

6. Understatement is preferred to overstatement. A plum tree is represented by a single spray; cat's whiskers by a few lines.

7. Don't fill the paper. As much should be implied as is actually stated.

8. When there is a lot to say, place the main action off the page and merely suggest it through the direction of a branch or a bird's glance.

9. Most subjects are painted at a middle distance, or closer. The exception is landscapes which are either an overview or flat and without perspective, like a maze in which the eye follows a path up the mountain or into the distance.

In each case I suggest trying the rule, and then its opposite, on whatever you paint. When you choose a new subject, look over this list to see which might apply to your painting. Then try several versions testing the truth of these "laws." In that way you will begin to incorporate through practice an understanding of what they mean.

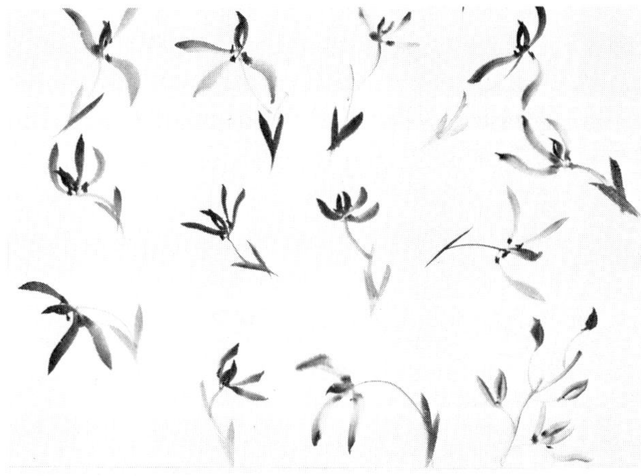

Orchid Flowers. There are many styles of orchid flowers, but all have five petals delicately shaded.

Chapter 7

MATERIALS

Brushes

Two major art forms in Japan and China, painting and calligraphy, employ what we call the Oriental brush. Based on the writing system, calligraphy is an exacting and much appreciated art in Japan. We in the West have nothing quite like it. As some calligraphy is usually included in an Oriental painting, in the signature and inscription, I have included an appendix on calligraphy.

The brushes employed by the two art forms are quite different. Both hold a lot of ink and taper to a point. But sumi-e brushes will tend to have softer hairs than calligraphy brushes, and they will hold their point better. This latter factor is the critical one. Sumi-e brushes must have resilience and be able to stand up and hold a fine point even after being brushed across the page many times.

Buying brushes may seem overly confusing (Look at all these brushes!) or overly simple (A brush is a brush!), but be sure to ask for a sumi-e brush or a painting brush as opposed to a calligraphy brush. Most of the brushes available in America are calligraphy brushes, but these are not good for painting (no matter what the store owner may tell you).

Several factors determine the cost of a brush, the most important being its ability (*a*) to keep a point and (*b*) to hold and provide an even flow of water onto the page. The quality of the materials and the workmanship are also important. Brush handles are usually of bamboo. The hairs of the brush could be deer, sheep, badger, or wolf, though other animals are used.

Buy two brushes, a large one and a small one.

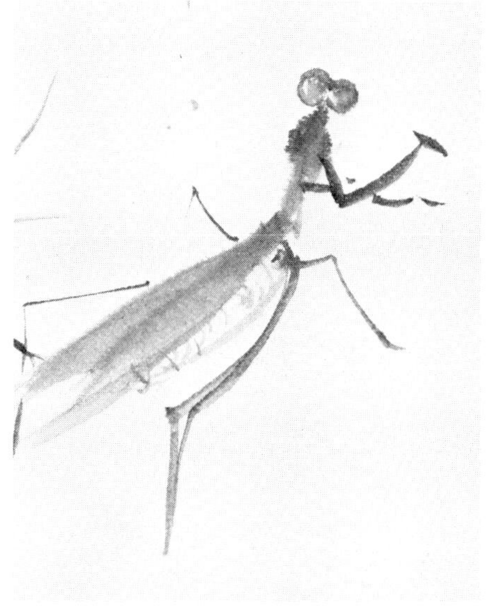

Praying Mantis.

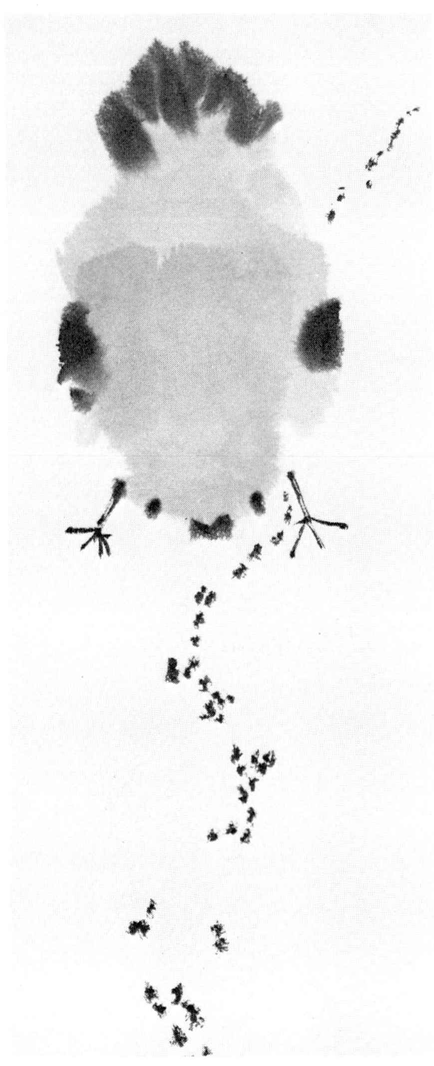

Chicks.

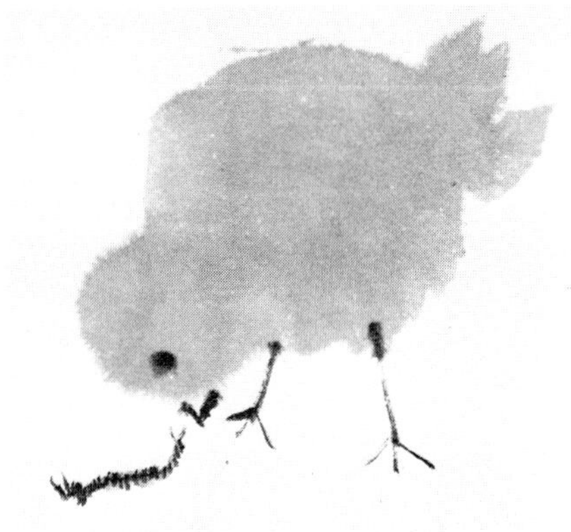

The hairs on the large one should be between 1-3/4 and 2 inches, that of the smaller about 3/4 inch. A medium size brush, maybe 1-1/4", could also be useful.

The more expensive brushes are not necessarily better than the less expensive, nor are they better for painting per se. Brushes made from the winter coats of deer, for example, are excellent for painting bamboo leaves, but they are not so good for general painting as are the less expensive brushes of sheep. For your first purchase, a large brush should cost $5 to $10, a small one about $2 to $5. After you paint for a while you may want to buy better brushes. You can expect to pay between $10 and $25 for a good large brush, and $5 to $10 for a small one. The best place to buy your first brushes is a Chinese or Japanese stationery store. Avoid buying an inexpensive "starter set"; the brushes are of poor quality. If you are buying an expensive brush, you have the right to insist on removing the sizing and trying the brush in the store to see if you like the feel of it and what it does on paper.

Preparing the brush for use is a matter of soaking the sized brush in water and stroking it firmly against the bottom of the container. The sizing melts and the brush becomes pliable in only a minute or two. Brushes are sized and bamboo caps are placed on the tips for protection against insects and damage during transportation. Once you remove the cap and soften the brush, do not replace the bamboo cap, as you may break hairs off. Instead, use a bamboo placemat to wrap the brushes. These are specially designed for the purpose. They are also inexpensive.

The proper care of brushes is important, because they are fragile. I never wash my brushes in the stream of water flowing directly from the tap, but instead fill a container with water and swish my brushes in it. When fresh water remains clear, I lift the brush out and squeeze the hairs into a shapely point. I never pull on the hairs. There are only so many hairs in a brush, and when a sufficient number has been pulled out, the entire head will fall out of the stem.

When removing the sizing or while painting, I
never tap the tip of the brush against the bottom
of the water container or against the paper towel.
This breaks hairs and will reduce your brush to a
stubby uselessness. Similarly, I never rotate or
rub the brush against a towel, as this breaks hairs.
And I never leave my brush in the water, because
this will loosen the glue holding the hairs to the
handle. The water also swells and cracks the bamboo, again causing the head to fall out.

Finally, I never leave my brushes uncleaned over-
night or even for a short time. While painting, I
clean each brush immediately after use. Dried ink
can be softened — but at the cost of broken bristles. (One exception is an inexpensive brush used
exclusively for calligraphy, where a firm brush is
sometimes desirable.)

A note on humidity and moisture. Bamboo
brushes have a tendency to crack in a dry climate.
There are two ways to inhibit this. One is to
maintain humidity by keeping your brushes in a
closed container with a moist rag. (This is done
also for ink sticks.) The second is to bind the end
of each brush near the bristles. This can be done
with tape. More effective is to carve a narrow
groove around the circumference of the brush and
wind nylon thread to secure it. Add a drop of
varnish or sealer to protect the thread. Some
brushes come this way when you buy them.

Special brushes are used for specific subjects or
effects. Wide brushes are for landscapes or mountains where washes are needed. Bamboo or reed
brushes create rough effects. Badger or deer [win-
ter coat] create smooth thin lines, as for bamboo
leaves, or rough textured lines if used against the
grain. Western brushes can sometimes be used
for special effects. The best brushes for general
use are made of wolf, sable, sheep, or the summer
coat of deer. Small brushes are useful for detail
work. It is rumored that there are brushes of a
single hair, taken from the armpit of a mouse, for
the finest work, as would be done on a mouse-
size miniature!

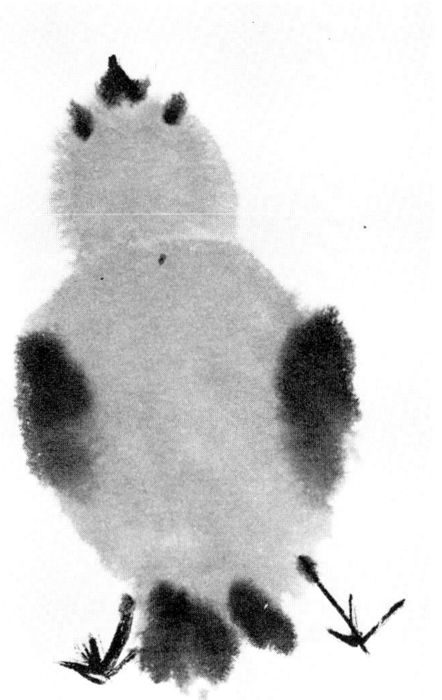

Fig. 36. A typical painting set-up includes brushes of various sizes, paper, a china bowl or plate for use as a palette, a water bowl, and an ink stone and ink stick. When painting the paper should be placed on a felt pad or a layer of newspapers to provide absorbency and lend spring to the paper. The mat at the left is for rolling the brushes to protect their points, the container on the upper right is to hold water for the ink stone, and on the lower right is a piece of cloth to absorb excess water from the brush while painting. The paperweight holds the paper.

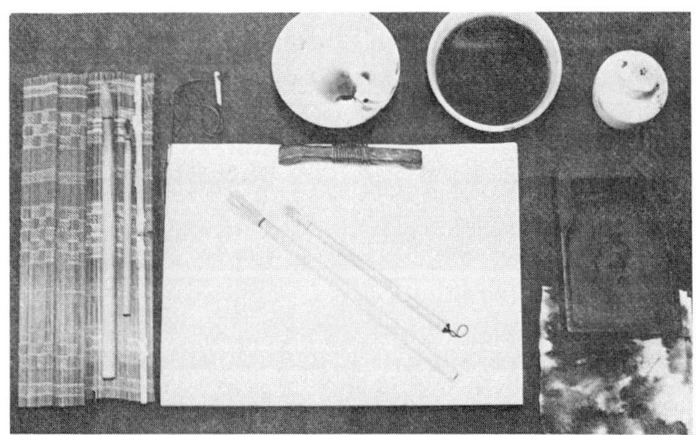

Fig. 37

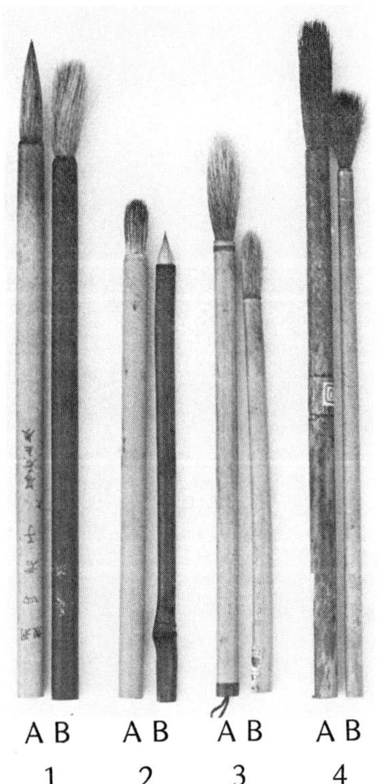

A B   A B   A B   A B
1   2   3   4

Brush Descriptions

The following brushes (*fude* or *shitsu*) are those generally used for sumi-e. I give their Japanese names and the type of hair as an aid in buying or ordering them.

1. *Tsuitate*, also called *mokkotsu* (boneless), is the basic sumi-e brush. If you buy one brush, this is it. It has a long handle, and the hairs are 1-3/4 or 2 inches long. A good one has hair that will snap back to its original shape after being twisted around the paper in various directions. Common hairs are badger, sheep, horse, and deer, usually the summer coats of these animals, and often in combination. The hairs are usually whitish in color, though badger is dark.

2. *Bokashi*, also called *kumadori* ("take a shadow") is a shading brush. A fat short-haired brush, it holds a lot of water. There are many varieties. Horse, deer, and sheep hair are most commonly used. These brushes are useful for shading in outlined paintings or for adding shading details to broad lines.

3. *Saishoku hitsu* (color brushes) come in many types, with short or long bristles, fat or narrow. They are soft and used to apply color details or to fill in outlines with color. They are made of two or three types of hair. The outside will be the belly hair of the horse, or from Chinese mountain sheep, and the inside will be sheep, badger, or deer. These brushes are inexpensive and quite good for all around painting.

4. Outline brushes are of three types:

a. *Shoyo* are used for drawing lines with a great deal of variation of thick and thin. They are usually made from sheep or mountain goat.

b. *Menso* ("front-face aspect") brushes are used for thin lines and adding bits of color. These are made from badger.

c. *Sokumyo* are used for elegant soft outlines. These brushes are made from sheep or white cat hair, or from badger, horse, or squirrel. This brush has longer, softer bristles than the *shoyo* brush.

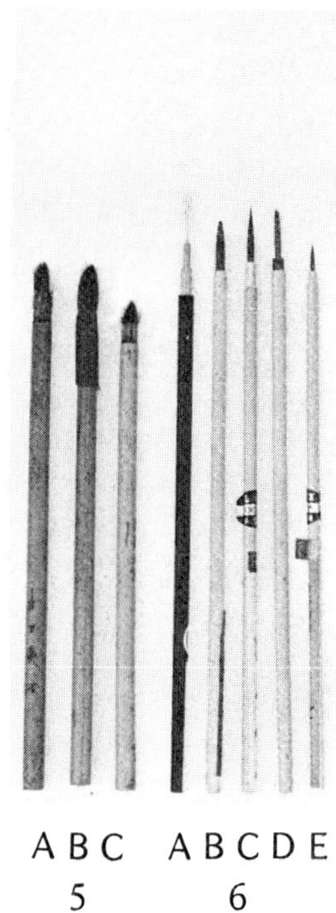

Fig. 37

Fig. 37. The variety of sumi-e brushes: (1) *Mokkotsu* brushes from Japan. *A* has a firmer bristle, from horse or goat; *B* has a softer bristle of sheep. (2) *Bokashi* or *kumadori* brushes from Japan. *A* is larger, made from deer; *B* is made from sheep. (3) *Saishoku* brushes from China. *A* is made in Peking, *B* in Shanghai. (4) *Shodo* brushes are usually employed in calligraphy, especially for large, rough work; they can be used similarly in painting, and sometimes for a powerful straight brush stroke. *A* is made of the winter coat of deer, *B* of badger. Both are rather expensive. (5) *Chinese shading brushes.* These inexpensive, small brushes, stiff or soft, are useful for most detail and for shading. *A* has horsehair in the center and goat around the outside. It is stiff and useful for fine lines. It holds a lot of ink for such a small brush. It can also be used for calligraphy. *B* and *C* are medium and small shading brushes, also useful for fine work. (6) *Menso* brushes from Japan. These are outline brushes, often used for landscapes. *A* is for very delicate lines, *B* for stronger or broader lines, *C* for thin and elegant lines, *D* for elegant lines, and *E* for fine lines. (7) *Hake* brushes from Japan. *A* is enamel coated, short bristled, of sheep hair. *B* has longer bristles. *C* is very wide. (8) *Shodo* brushes. Like 4*A* and *B*, these brushes can be used for calligraphy or rough painting work. *A* is made from a reed and *B* from a piece of bamboo. The ends are shredded or splintered fiber, an organic part of the brush and not pasted or added on. This produces rough, naturalistic, "purist" work.

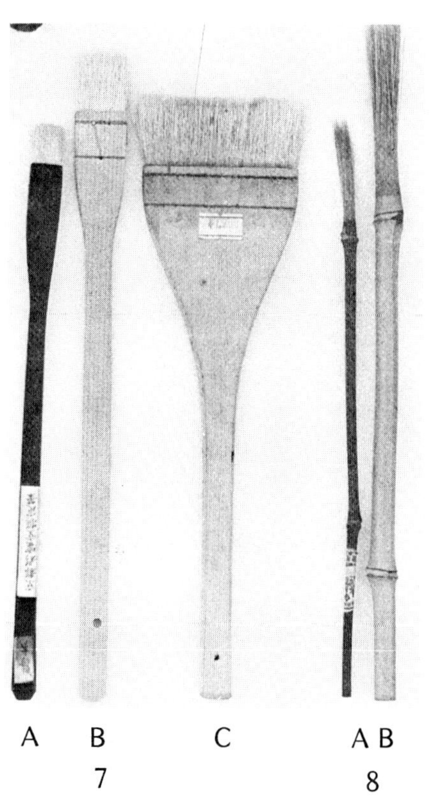

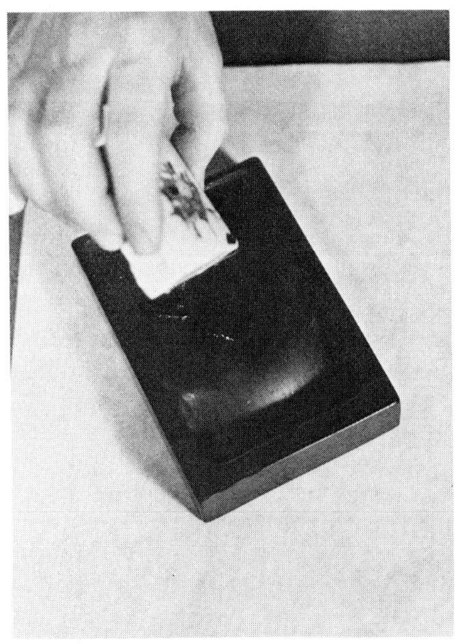

Fig. 38. Water is placed on the *suzuri* (ink stone). Either fill the well with the amount you feel you want to use or add a little at a time as you grind it.

Fig. 39. The ink stick is rubbed against the surface of the stone in large, free, circular movements. The pressure will cause the ink to blend with the water, producing a thick dark ink.

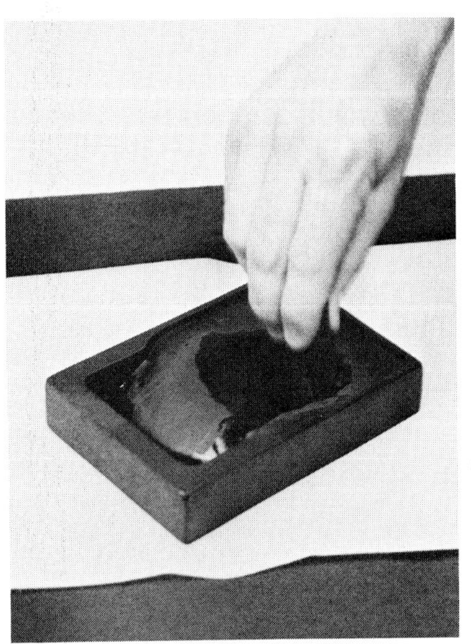

5. *Hake* (*hake* means brush; *sumi no hake* will distinguish it from brushes used to paint houses!) is a wide brush, between 15 and 300 mm. It is made from combinations like hair from horse belly and the summer coat of deer or horsehair and sheep. It is used for washes and shading, as for mountains in the background.

6. *Renpitsu* (composite or continuous brush) is also used for washes or painting background areas. It is made of several brushes, either *tsuitate* or color brushes, put together in a row of three, five, or seven brushes.

A Note on Using One Brush

Often one brush is used for both rough and detailed work, for washes and fine lines, even for wet and dry effects. Most sumi-e is done quickly, and using one or two brushes helps preserve the integrity of the brush work. In one school of sumi-e, an entire picture is painted with one brush load of ink, the finer and darker work done with the black-inked tip of the brush, the lighter strokes and washes done when the ink begins to run out.

Ink Sticks and Ink Stone

The ink you use will reflect your mood, and the feeling you want to project in your painting. Some inks have a blue tinge, others are reddish-brown in hue. The former lend a cool clearness to your painting, the latter a warm strength. You may want to use Chinese or Japanese liquid ink, the kind commonly used for calligraphy practice. It is a thick black ink, containing glue. It will not fade like our common fountain pen ink. With it, you may simply plunge right in and start painting as the impulse moves you.

Ink sticks come from Japan and China. Like dried or powdered watercolor pigments, dried ink sticks are a convenient way of storing and transporting a potentially messy substance. Ink sticks are made by burning pine or vegetable matter in a small room, scraping the resultant carbon from the ceiling, and pressing it into sticks. Lampblack is also used. Often a design or writing is embossed or painted on the stick to indicate the quality and characteristics of the ink.

Black can have many different tones — red, vermillion, blue, purple, and so on. I know of at

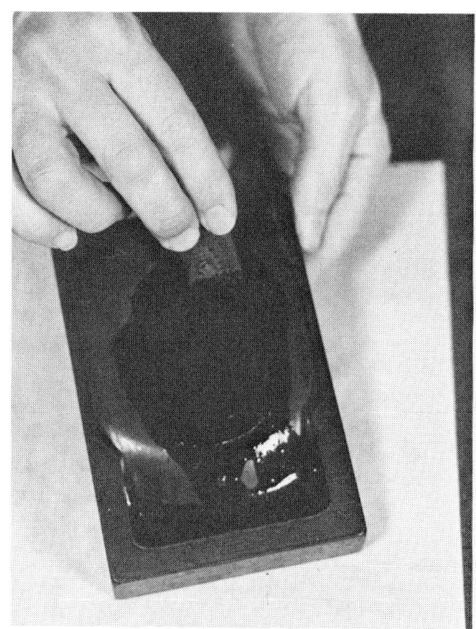

Fig. 40. (above) When the ink is rich and black, scrape it into the well. Then draw more water up to the surface of the stone, or pour more on, and continue grinding until you have two or three teaspoonsful of the blackest ink you desire.

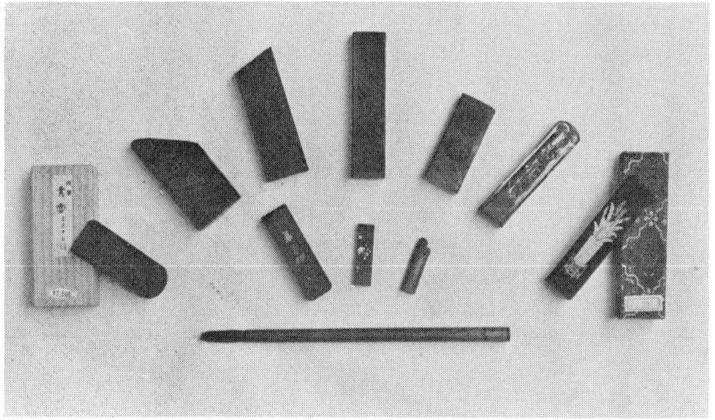

Fig. 41. (above) Ink sticks come in a variety of shapes and sizes. The Japanese ink at left is blue tinted, the Chinese ink at right is red tinted. Ink is available in colors, also. The smallest stick here is actually red.

Fig. 42. (below) Ink sticks are often decorated with calligraphy or pictures, and they are usually painted as well.

Fig. 43. (below) *Suzuris* (ink stones) come in many shapes and sizes and often have covers. The stone on the right is from China, the one on the left from Korea, and the one with the brush from Korea. The rest are from Japan. The small spoon on the center stone is used to place water on the stone.

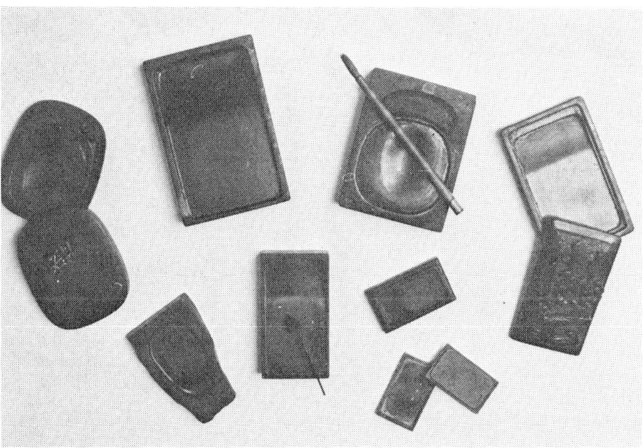

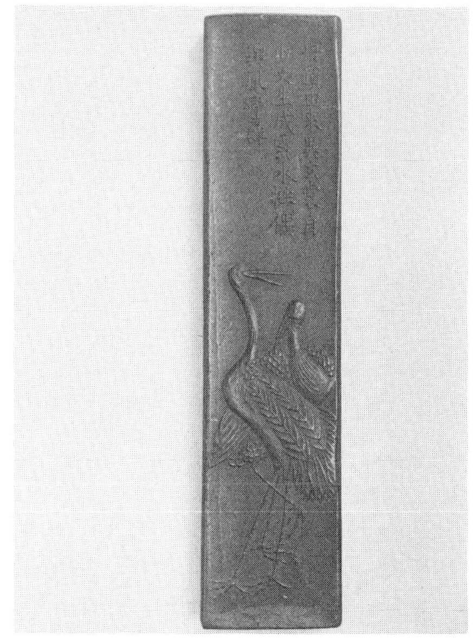

least thirty different black inks, each possessing a different tone. Any pleasing inexpensive ink will do, however, at the start. Later you may find one ink you particularly like. When buying ink, keep in mind that most Japanese ink is blue-toned, while much of the Chinese ink is red or brown in tone.

Suzuris, or ink stones, are shaped especially for grinding ink. They have a flat surface upon which the ink stick is rubbed, along with some water, to produce liquid ink. The surface of the stone slopes gradually to a shallow well, in which the ground ink collects for use.

The best ink stones come from Tankei Province, in mainland China. Good ones are also found in Japan, on Shikoku Island and near Hiroshima. Each *suzuri* is carved from a single stone. If you have good quality ink, a good stone will grind your ink smoothly and quickly. If the grain is too small, it will take too long to grind the ink. If the grain is too large, chunks of ink will be broken off during grinding, and the ink will be gritty instead of smooth. Both these problems are aggravated by using poor quality ink. *Suzuris* are generally grey-black in color. Do not buy a stone that is pressed into a mold from powdered rock chips, or one made of metal, wood, porcelain, or paper.

Grinding one's ink is traditional in painting, as well as in calligraphy. The ink stick is rubbed against the stone with some water. Grinding can take anywhere from a few minutes to a half hour, depending on the quality and grain of the stone and the ink, and upon the quantity of ink and the degree of blackness desired. The ink can be ground either forward and backward, or in a circular motion. If only a small amount is desired, then only a teaspoonful of water is necessary. If you will be painting for a couple of hours or more, you will probably want to make three or four teaspoonfuls of ink. When the well of ink is thick, rich, and black, it is ready. Test it on your paper. You should be able to produce the blackest color you

will need in one stroke, without having to paint
over it twice.

Grinding ink has been elevated to an almost sac-
red ritual in Japan and China, an essential preparation for the coming work of painting. It suggests
the Zen attitude that performing menial tasks
can bring enlightenment. Grinding ink requires
time and patience, rather than effort. And as any
craftsperson knows, taking your time can be a
meditation in its own right.

Although you will usually grind your ink ahead
of time, sometimes you may want to grind as you
paint, a little at a time as you need it. This can
interrupt your rhythm and slow you down, however, and it is not practical when you are doing
wet paintings requiring speedy application of
inky layers.

Ink is taken directly from the *suzuri*. This has
a tendency to quickly dilute the ink in the well,
as the brush is usually full of water. You will
have to renew the strength of your ink occasionally as you paint. You will find it useful, in addition, to have a dish for use as a palette to mix
shades of grey. This can also be used to make up
a large quantity of a specific shade for use as a
wash or for a large painting.

Ink stick and ink stone can be purchased relatively inexpensively, though good quality materials can be expensive. Ink sticks are available
from about $2 and up. Price is usually a good in-
dication of quality. Good ink is available for less
than $10, and truly excellent ink can be gotten
from sticks that range in price from $10 to $20.
Except in the case of old ink — where you are
buying an antique and, perhaps, a quality no
longer available — there is no need to go higher.
Ink sticks need not be expensive to suit your
taste and needs.

Ink stones are another matter. Inexpensive
student-grade stones are available for as little as
$2. You should probably begin with a stone cost-
ing $5 to $10. Choose one that is about three
inches by five inches in size. Better stones are

somewhat more difficult to come by. You will
have to pay between $50 and $100 for a large-
size, good-quality stone. Avoid elaborately carved
stones, because you are not necessarily getting
good quality and you are paying for the decoration.

Ink stones must be washed after each use. If
left to dry, the ink will leave a crusty residue that
will slowly build up, held firmly by the glue the
ink contains. This is hard to remove, and it will
reduce the quality of any ink you grind. Frag-
ments of dried ink, when picked up by the brush,
will produce undesirable smears. Be careful not
to drop your ink stone, as it breaks easily. Even
a sharp rap can cause a hairline crack which will
allow the ink to leak out.

Ink sticks, like brushes, tend to become brittle
and crack because there is so much less humidity
here than in Japan. If you anticipate a problem
with this, keep your ink sticks in a closed container along with a damp cloth. When the cloth is
dry, rewet it. This will provide the proper moisture conditions.

Paper

The variety of Japanese, Chinese, and Korean
paper suitable for sumi-e is immense. Several
kinds are imported to this country. Much of it
is hand-made and quite expensive, although the
sheets are quite large. Machine-made paper
is less expensive and of sufficient quality for your
purposes, especially when you first begin. Avoid
using scrap paper once you start producing paintings you like. There is nothing more frustrating
than discovering you have painted your best picture on newsprint, which will turn yellow in six
months.

Most Oriental paper is called "rice paper." This
is a misnomer. Most of the paper is made from the
inner bark of mulberry or other fruit trees. Sometimes it is made from rice plant fiber, hemp, or a
combination including cotton. Oriental paper is

sized with a mixture of alum and glue. Papers will
have varying degrees of absorbency; glazed, semi-
absorbent, and absorbent. You will find a particular absorbency which you and your brush work
well with. Personal preference and the demands
of your subject will determine which paper you
use. All papers have one "shiny" side and one
rough side, though it is sometimes difficult to tell
the difference. Paint is usually applied to the
smoother, shiny surface, though a softer effect
can sometimes be created by using the rough side.

Paper comes in rolls, tablets, and sheets. Rolls
come in 6", 10", 12", 15", and 18" widths. These
are good for scroll style paintings. Tablets, usually called "sumi-e sketch paper," are available in
sizes ranging from about 8" x 12" to about 15"
x 36". Rolls and tablets cost from $2 to $6, depending on the size. Sheets of paper measure 12"
x 60", 24" x 60", 24" x 36", and numerous other
sizes. Japanese paper is not made in consistent
sizes. Sheets run anywhere from 50¢ to $3 or $4
per sheet and higher.

Other Materials

In addition to brushes, ink, and paper you will
need a water container, a dish to use as a palette,
a cloth or paper towel to wipe the brushes and absorb excess water, and some newspaper or a felt

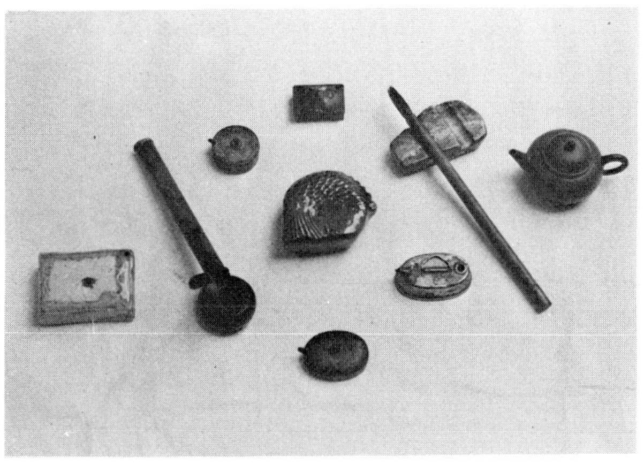

Fig. 44. Many novel designs are employed in making water containers.
The central fish-shaped container
comes from Korea; the "teapot" is
actually a container; and the upper-
most one depicts a baseball pitcher.
The brush is placed against a brush
rest. The other object is a traveling
calligraphy set (see Fig. 45).

Fig. 45. Old-fashioned traveling calligraphy set. The pen was kept in
the handle, and the ink was held in
a cloth ball in the hollow bell. The
lid kept the ink from evaporating
(less of a problem in humid Japan
than in the United States). The
whole was tucked into the belt.

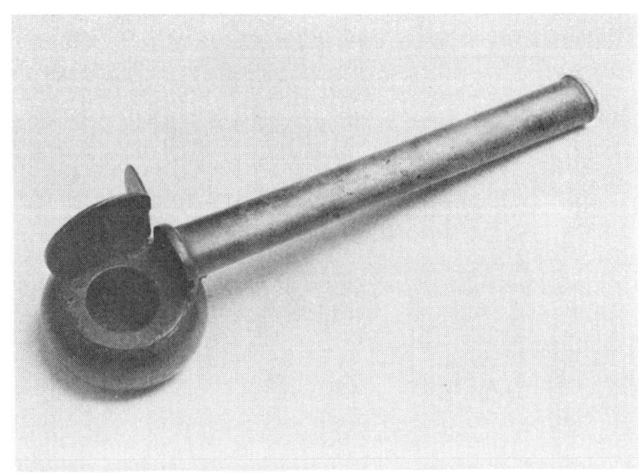

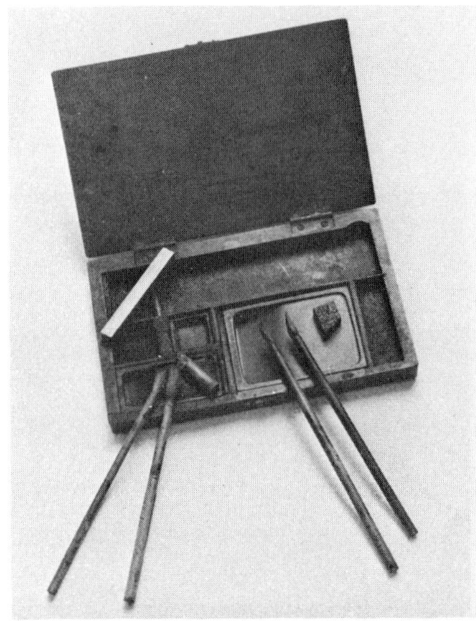

Fig. 46. Traveling sumi-e sets made
it possible to carry the tools of painting out of the studio. Short-handled
brushes, a paperweight, a compartment for a seal, and two ink stones,
one red and one black, make up this
simple, beautiful set.

Fig. 47. Painting boxes for storing
materials or transporting them, like
this one, usually have a compartment
at the top with a lid, and two drawers. Ink and *suzuri,* brushes and seals
can be kept in the top for easy access while painting. Extra materials
can be stored in the drawers.

pad upon which to paint. You will probably want
a bamboo mat to roll up your brushes, and a box
to carry everything in. There are many additional
accessories, such as water pourers and brush rests,
but these are not essential.

Seals and inscription. When a painting is completed, it is signed by brush in characters (Japanese or Chinese), and a seal is added. The signature
is often a poetic name, or a symbol the painter
uses in place of a name. You can find out how to
write your name in Kanji characters or Katakana
script from someone who writes Japanese, perhaps even a Japanese language manual. Most signatures are two characters in length, representing
the initial sounds or syllables of your family name.

Seals can be ordered from Japan, though there
are some seal carvers in this country. Seals made

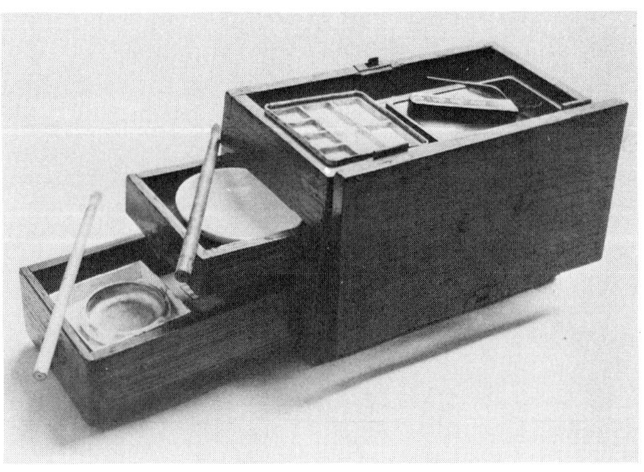

here will cost $20 to $50; those made in Japan anywhere from $4 to $25 *per character!* The characters are carved in stone, and sometimes in bamboo or another substance. Seal signatures usually bear the painter's name. But sometimes a poetic or witty phrase will be used in place of, or in addition to, the name. The characters are generally in an old style.

It is traditional to place the signature and seal in the least conspicuous part of the painting, so that it adds to the rhythm yet doesn't attract attention. The signature is placed first, and the seal is placed below it. Often two seals will be used, one "masculine" and one "feminine" (depending on whether the letters are raised or recessed). Sometimes another seal, chosen to make a comment of either a humorous or serious nature, is placed at the beginning of the inscription or near the top of the painting. Western artists occasionally print their names above or below the seal. A seal reproducing Western "initials" can also be used.

The inscription is written as a commentary on the painting. If the painting is commemorative of a specific occasion, or is a gift, the inscription will make reference to this. Often the inscriptions are poetic or symbolic. Poems are even used. Dates, places, and names can be included, though

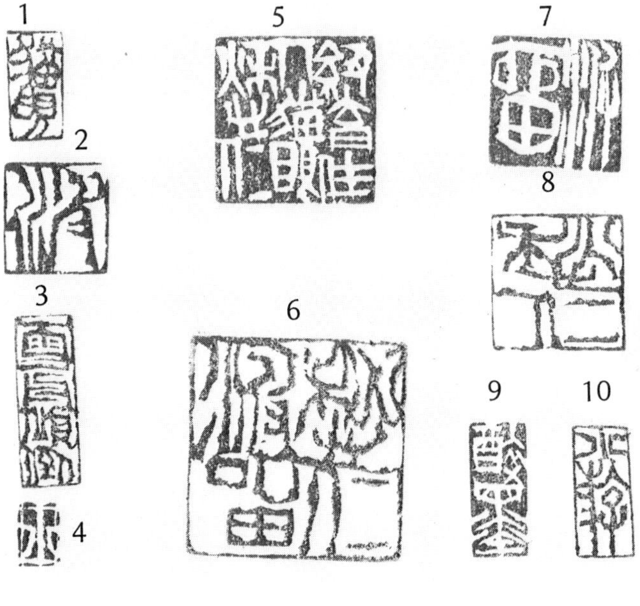

Seals. These seals were made as a set, the characters carved in an old style. The two seals at upper right represent my first and last names. Much care must be taken when choosing a name. The meaning must be consistent with the dignity and intention you wish to convey. Having a complete set allows you to choose seals that suit the size and style of the painting.

Translations are: (1) "Cat's Eyes," the nearest approximation in Japanese to "hazel-eyed." (2) "Po," which stands for Paul. (3) "Leaning on Sesshu," which refers to my liking and indebtedness to the fifteenth-century painter Sesshu Toyo (1420-1506). (4) "Small," the meaning of Paul in English. (5) "New York Foreigner; Cat's Eyes Foreigner," which is a kind of identifying seal that would be used at the top of paintings. (6) "Shu-jin Poru," which is my name. (7) "Poru," my first name. (8) "Shu-jin," my last name. The Japanese rendering has the first syllable of my family name "Siu" (pronounced "shoe") and the second syllable "dzin" (pronounced "gene"). The first character has two parts, for "autumn" and "heart," and is translated "the sweet yearning of autumn." The second is translated "the virtue of the human heart." (9) "Drunk with Ink," which is a humorous seal indicating my love for painting. (10) "Small Play," another humorous seal with a pun on my name.

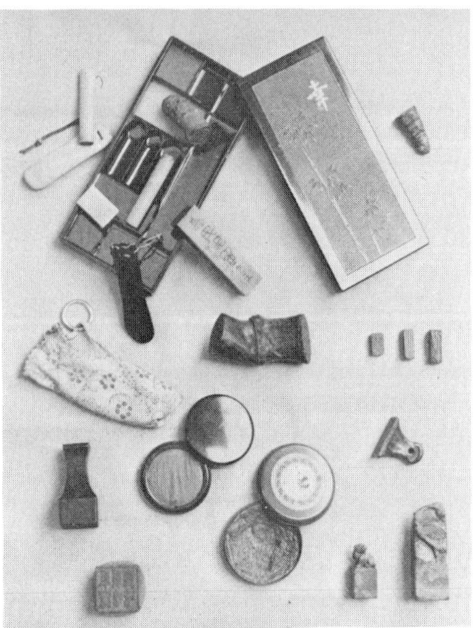

Fig. 48. A variety of seals made from wood, bamboo, metal, and stone. The two round boxes contain the seal paste, red in color and made from cinnabar. The pouches are to hold the seals and, perhaps, a small paste container. The seal above the paste boxes is made from a bamboo root. The three small seals to the right are of stone, and below them is one of metal. Two carved stone seals are at the lower right. The large box is a modern plastic sumi-e kit.

these will all be written with characters. In the case of a Western artist, an English inscription is sometimes used.

The Appendix contains a list of inscriptions that can be used with your paintings. If you look over this list you will get an idea of what is considered appropriate for a short general inscription. If you want to make longer inscriptions for specific occasions, a friend's birthday or wedding, for example, you will have to get someone who writes Japanese to write it out in characters. You can then practice it and add it when you can brush all the characters well.

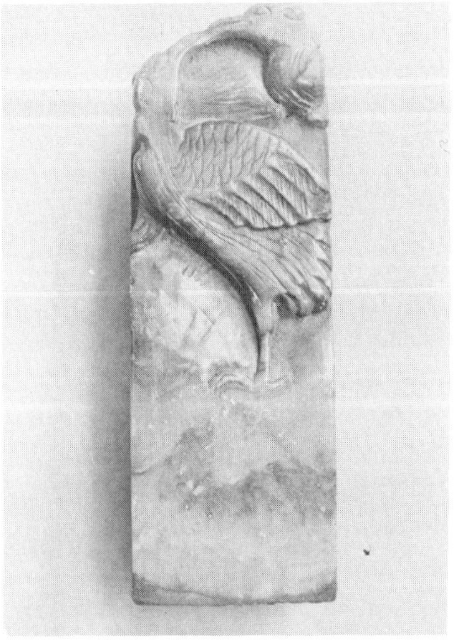

Fig. 49. This seal is carved from stone and decorated with a phoenix, the symbol of long life.

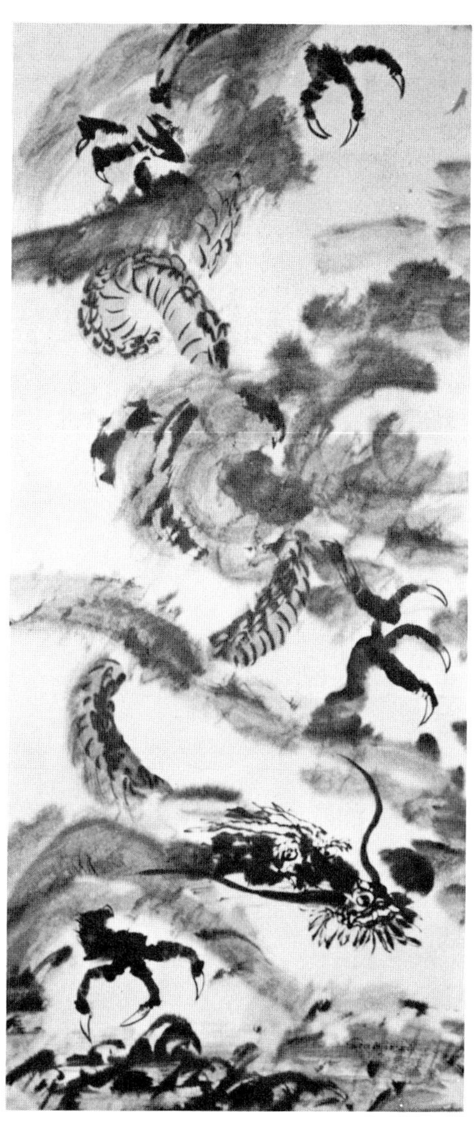

Sign of the Dragon. The dragon is the supreme being in the mythology of Japan, challenged only by the tiger (there are no elephants in Japan). Dragons are almost always surrounded by stormy clouds or seas. They are snakelike, scaly, have four legs and spume fire and smoke. But they are actually symbolic of good fortune and wisdom.

Appendix

Daffodil Morning. This painting is a haiga,
which combines poetry (*hai,* as in *haiku*)
and painting (*ga,* as in *suiboku-ga*). Poetry
painting is an outgrowth of zen calligraphy,
where the pictorial aspects are an extension
and explication of the calligraphic text. This
haiga was a combined effort between shodo
artist Sharon Nakazato and myself.
Nakazato is vice-president of the Haiku
Society of America. The occasion for the
collaboration was a class on haiga. I painted
the daffodils first, and Nakazato created an
impromptu haiku. It translates, "Hey,
daffodil! Show me your face — smiling."
Notice the strong use of "color" in the
painting, and the similar "colored" brush
stroke used in the calligraphy.

CALLIGRAPHY

Oriental painting and calligraphy (*shodo* in Japanese) are related, yet they are as different from each other as are classical music and jazz. Although the approach of *A Meditation in Ink* can be applied to both arts, the strokes and the criteria for analysis and appreciation are entirely different. Whereas in painting we strive to capture a feeling or "moment" in a striking though familiar image, calligraphy seeks to express that feeling or "moment" in a perfection of style, balance, and phrasing.

The Chinese and Japanese writing systems are the basis of the art of calligraphy. Thus every school child in the East absorbs something of this ancient art while learning the ABC's. Striving to make good characters, endeavoring to make each the same size, memorizing the nuances and subtleties of meaning behind each character, students learn indirectly some of the criteria for appreciation and understanding of the calligrapher's art. And because they use brush and ink, they also learn something of the painter's art.

Every Oriental painter possesses a passing familiarity with the principles of calligraphy. Unless you have studied an Oriental language, chances are that the characters and the method of writing are not familiar to you. This short introduction will help you to learn enough to sign your name and write a few simple inscriptions on your paintings.

There are many styles of calligraphy, each using different character forms, some rough and informal, others stylized, courtly or finished. Some are hieroglyphic forms, others follow the latest trends in abstraction or realism.

Calligraphy is usually done with a calligraphy

brush, though it is quite acceptable to use your sumi-e brush for signatures and inscriptions on paintings. This will help preserve the unity of the painting. Overall, the writing should complement the spacing and rhythm of the painting, and the style should also be consistent with the style and intent of the painting.

Characters are formed from certain basic strokes which can be practiced. And there is an order of placing the strokes, which also conforms to certain general rules. Good calligraphic characters are well spaced and attractive; they are balanced individually and are of a consistent size. All parallel strokes, both horizontal and vertical, are evenly spaced, so the whole character is balanced and in proportion.

After you have learned the basic strokes, you are ready to go on to inscriptions. On the next few pages are inscriptions selected and brushed by Sharon Nakazato, a Japanese-trained *shodo* artist. Practice them. The most important thing to keep in mind is to make each character the same size regardless of the number of strokes.

Stroke order follows the general order of left to right and top to bottom. There are some common stroke patterns which turn up again and again, and as you practice you will acquire a sense

---

Calligraphy Practice. Figure A is the character for "long-lasting" or "eternal," an excellent character for practice as it contains six different strokes. Figure B shows the stroke order and direction. Column I illustrates six basic strokes. Column II shows four simple characters for practicing the basic strokes (translations, top to bottom: "middle"; "person"; "generation" or "decade"; "the source"). Columns III and IV illustrate the stroke order and direction for these basic strokes and characters.

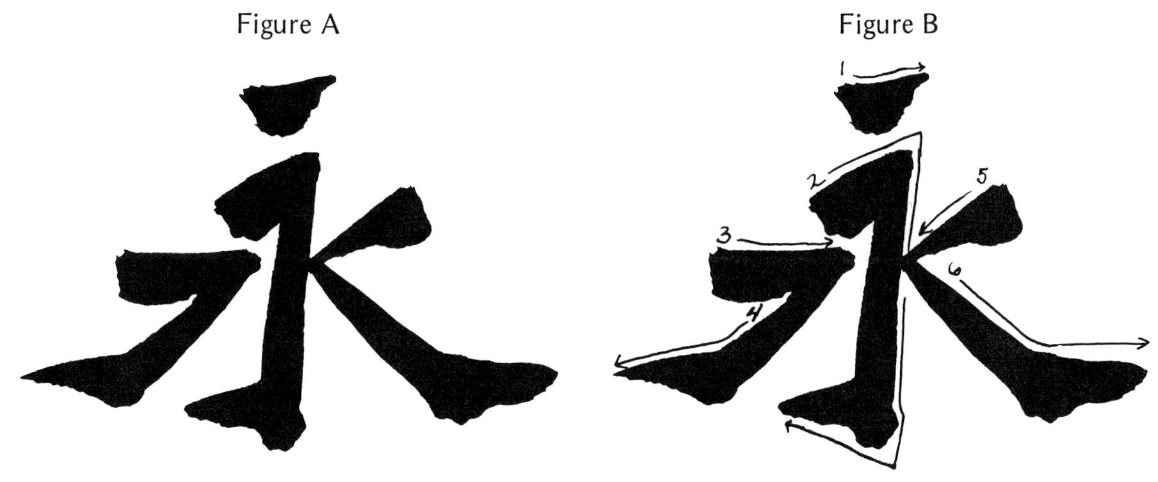

Figure A
Figure B
I
II
III
IV

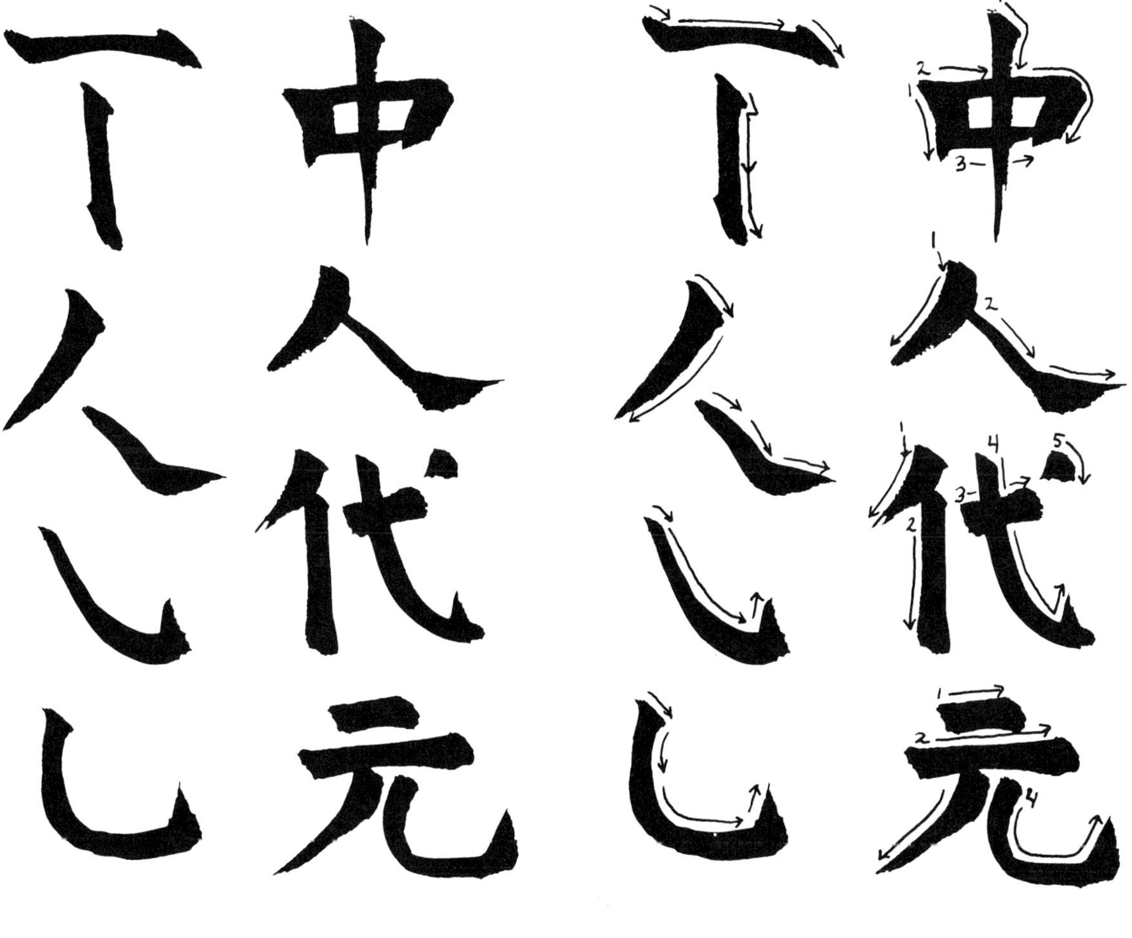

V	VI	VII
菊	菊	菊
蘭	蘭	蘭
松	松	松
竹	竹	竹
風	風	風
如	如	如
空	空	空

Calligraphy Practice (*cont'd*). Column V gives
seven of the most common characters used in the
inscriptions (translations, top to bottom: "chrysanthemum"; "orchid"; "pine"; "bamboo";
"wind"; "like" or "as"; "emptiness" or "the void").
Column VI demonstrates some basic principles
of calligraphic composition: (1) vertical symmetry,
(2) horizontal symmetry, (3) over-all balance, (4)
variation in balance, (5) even spacing of parallel
lines, (6) balance of left and right, and (7) even
spacing of elements. (Note that each character,
no matter its shape or the number of strokes, takes
the same amount of space.) Column VII demonstrates stroke order for the seven characters. Note
that brushing, like script, is not inflexibly square,
like typewriting. After mastering the basic principles of symmetry and balance, one works to develop an individual style which is reflected in variations in the elements of the characters. The tension between symmetry and asymmetry enhances
the beauty of the forms.

---

of "stroke order" that will enable you to analyze
how to write new characters.

    For calligraphy practice you can buy special
pre-ruled paper. You can also fold rice paper into blocks. Or you can follow any ruled vertical
lines. As with many things, practice is the key
to facility!

6	5	4	3	2	1

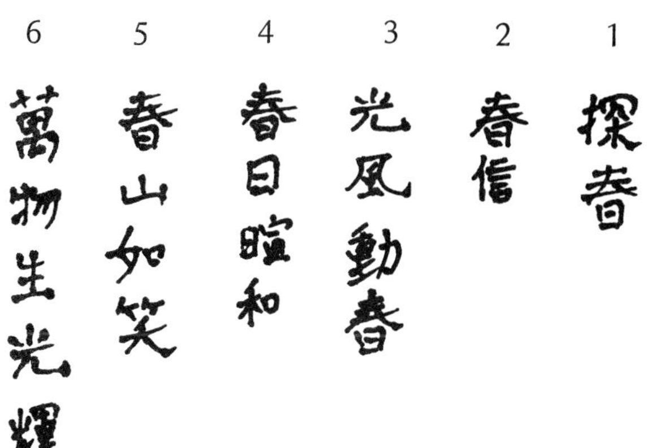

SPRING

1   seeking spring
2   tidings of spring
       (flowers, birds, etc.)
3   the leaves glisten after a rain,
       touched by the wind bringing
       spring
4   warm and soft spring days
5   the mountains in spring seem
       to laugh
6   all things come alive (with light)

7   the birds play in the forest, fill-
    ing the spring with sound

SUMMER

8   inviting coolness; a fan
9   wandering about and having fun
10   the long leisurely days
11   escaping the heat in the cool
     breezes through the bamboo
     grove

AUTUMN

12   the voice of autumn (the wind)
13   after autumn dreams
14   reflections of autumn leaves
15   autumn moves the heart
16   autumn fruits from spring
     blossoms
17   skies are cool and clear, and
     everyone feels strong and healthy

WINTER

18   the green of evergreens in winter
19   winter buds
20   snowflakes fall in winter before
     flower petals (bloom and fall)
     in spring
21   appreciating the sun in winter
     (loving the good in people)
22   winter has come, bringing a quiet
     of endless fascination

LANDSCAPE

23   landscape with clouds (a peaceful
     world; a prosperous nation)
24   hold the moon in your heart
     (have a pure heart)

12	11	10	9	8	7
秋聲	避暑竹風涼	永日暇	遊渉	招涼	林間鳥弄春音

18	17	16	15	14	13
晚翠	天涼人健	春花秋實	感人	映紅楓	秋夢後

24	23	22	21	20	19
抱月	景雲	冬來幽興長	冬日可愛	雪先花	冬芽

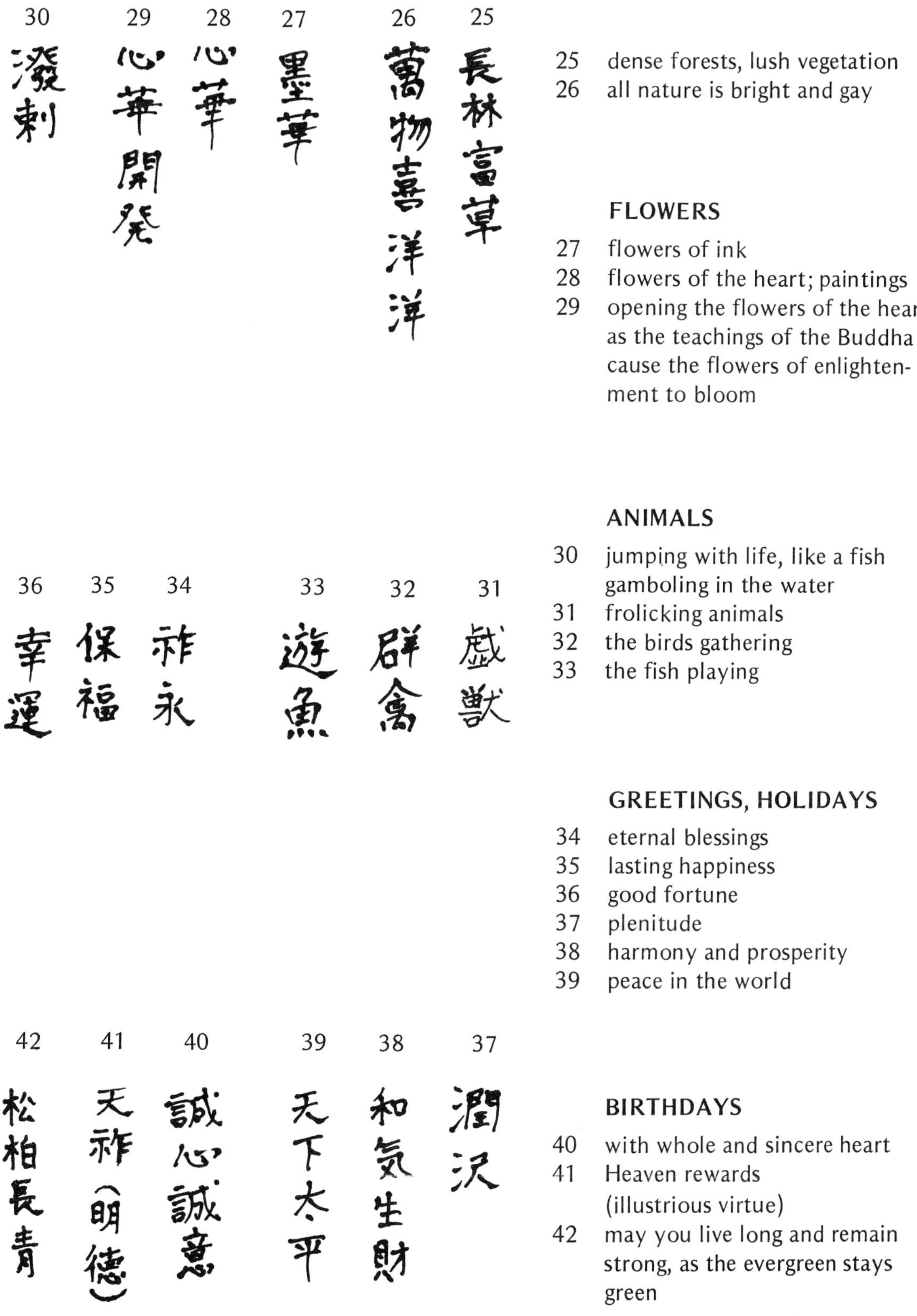

25 dense forests, lush vegetation
26 all nature is bright and gay

FLOWERS

27 flowers of ink
28 flowers of the heart; paintings
29 opening the flowers of the heart; as the teachings of the Buddha cause the flowers of enlightenment to bloom

ANIMALS

30 jumping with life, like a fish gamboling in the water
31 frolicking animals
32 the birds gathering
33 the fish playing

GREETINGS, HOLIDAYS

34 eternal blessings
35 lasting happiness
36 good fortune
37 plenitude
38 harmony and prosperity
39 peace in the world

BIRTHDAYS

40 with whole and sincere heart
41 Heaven rewards (illustrious virtue)
42 may you live long and remain strong, as the evergreen stays green

43 long life, wealth, and honor

BIRTH OF CHILD

44 born under a good star, he/she
will prosper

NEW HOUSE

45 peace and prosperity
in the home

NEW JOB OR BUSINESS

46 praying for your good fortune
47 success in the new enterprise
48 success in the new enterprise

THANKS

49 thankfulness

PRESENT

50 (a gift) humbly proffered

NEW YEAR'S

51 greeting spring
52 good wishes on the New Year

ZENISMS

53 the clear mirror - the Zen mind
54 seek life in death (seek enlightenment through awareness of death,
through an aware death, through
awareness of now)
55 the dragon chants through
the withered tree
56 the willow fluff follows the
wind, without attachment
57 though the current be swift, it
cannot sweep away the moon
58 one in true meditation (samadhi)
feels the heat of flames as cool
59 the aged pines and the hidden
birds all speak Truth

48	47	46	45	44	43
生意意興業	成功立業	折吉祥	家内安全	吉星高照	長命富貴

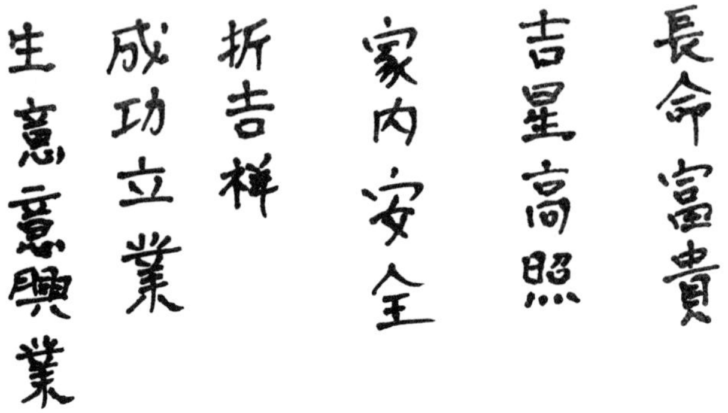

54	53	52	51	50	49
死中求浩	鏡清	賀正	迎春	謹呈	感謝

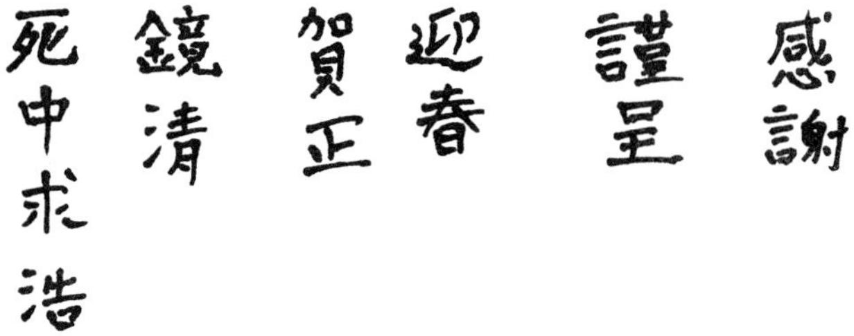

59	58	57	56	55
幽鳥弄眞如　古松談般若	滅却心頭火自涼	水急不流月	柳絮随風	枯木龍吟

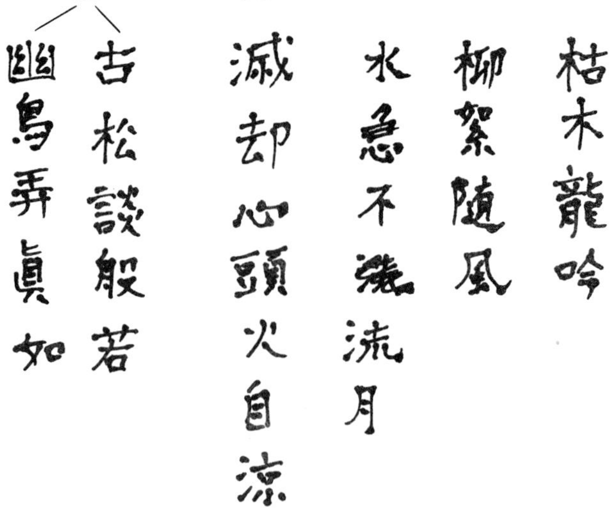

65	64	63	62	61	60
潑墨	醉墨	悦目	游心	游芸	小遊

MISCELLANEOUS

60 small play
61 having fun with art
62 relaxing with ink
63 giving pleasure to the eye
64 drunk with ink
65 splashed ink
66 treasure without end
67 free and easy; leisurely,
    without a care

71	70	69	68	67	66
繁菊照深居	菊有精神	菊凌霜	賞菊	悠悠自適	無盡寶

CHRYSANTHEMUMS

68 appreciating chrysanthemums
69 chrysanthemum blooms
    withstand the frost
70 chrysanthemums have a spirit
    of their own
71 chrysanthemums blooming in
    profusion brighten the darkest
    parts of the house

PINE

72 the pine and bamboo make music
73 the wind through the pines
    cleanses the heart
74 virtuous conduct; vigorous old age

77	76	75	74	73	72
蘭在幽林亦自香	蘭有秀（菊有芳）	蘭竹潤	松柏節操	松風洗心	松竹今題

ORCHIDS

•75 orchid and bamboo richly laden
    with moisture (like the brush)
76 the orchid is known for its ele-
    gance (the chrysanthemum for
    its perfume)
77 in the peace and quiet of the
    forest, the orchid easily releases
    its fragrance (the mind at rest
    is naturally enlightened)

78 virtue - like the fragrance of
an orchid
79 orchid words - the words of
a true friend
80 relationship with a true friend -
like orchid fragrance

BAMBOO

81 a heart honest and straight
as bamboo
82 deep, quiet bamboo grove
(peace of meditation)
83 the sound of wind rustling
bamboo leaves; a flute
84 spiritual strength of bamboo
(it is not subdued by frost)
85 bamboo grove pavilion
(very poetic)
86 bamboo in rain, bamboo in wind
87 you must have bamboo in your
mind (heart) before you can
paint it
88 as in splitting bamboo (starting
is the hardest part)
89 in the still deeps of the mountains, the bamboo sings

The inscriptions on this page were painted with a calligraphy brush, unlike those on the preceding pages,
made for clarity of stroke with a Pentel pen.

THE COLORS OF BLACK AND WHITE

Students (especially the art students), are often surprised when I talk about a black and white painting as having "color." "Are you referring to tone?" they ask. What I mean by color, however, is closer to the meaning the word has in music. Color in sumi-e sparks your attention and tantalizes your senses by highlighting areas of the painting at the same time as it provides contrast.

Beginning students, I have found, usually are hesitant to use strong contrasts of dark ink and light ink. The resulting paintings are often mono-colored, uniformly grey with no "highs" or "lows." Achieving color in sumi-e requires using some very black lines and some very light ones. This is especially important for creating a sense of depth or distance.

To imbue your work with aliveness, however, means more than simply having dark and light in a painting. Each brush stroke must have some color, as well. This can be realized with every brushload of ink by touching the side, sometimes the tip, to the very dark ink on the flat surface of the suzuri. In practice, once you have charged your brush with its basic coloration — whether light or medium ink makes no difference — simply touch the side of the brush to the stone, picking up some dark ink on the bristles along one edge. I often grind some extra ink before beginning a new painting, ensuring a handy supply of dark ink with which to color the side of my brush.

The wetness of the brush will largely determine the extent to which the "touch" of black ink will influence the brush stroke's color. It is the water that causes the ink to flow. Thus, a dry brush will pick up only a small amount of ink from the suzuri's surface, giving your brush stroke a slight, sharp edge of tonation. The water in a wet brush, however, will

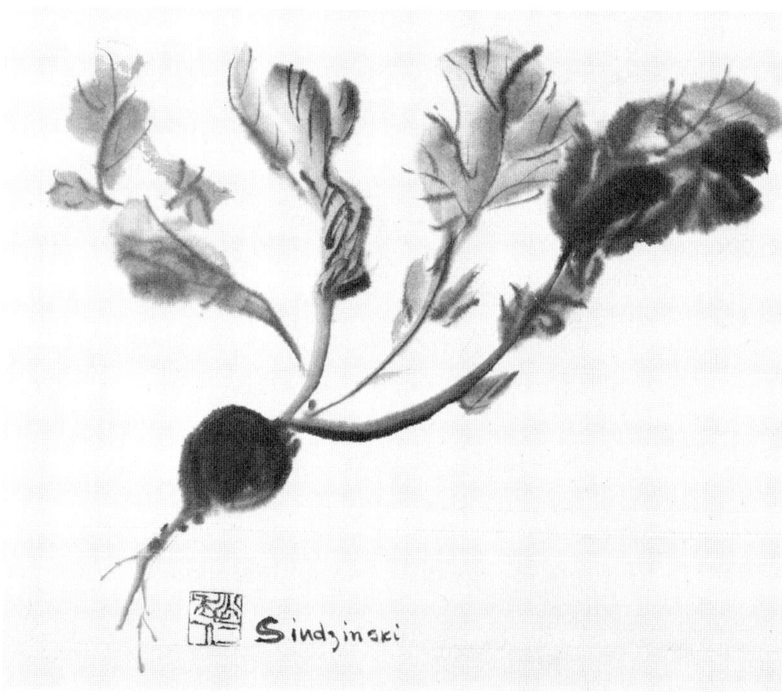

Radish. A humble subject, truly. But when capturing the colors of black and white, we go directly back to the basics.

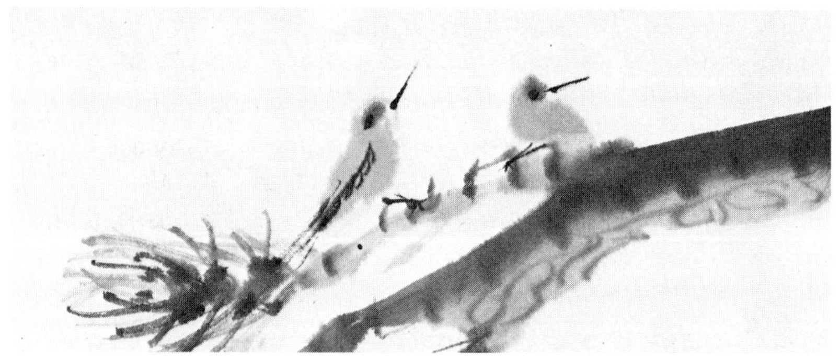

Out on a Limb. The colors of black and white should be clear, not muddy. Avoid using too many shades of ink in a brush load or too much water on the brush.

pull more of the ink farther into the fibers, resulting in a strongly blotted stroke. To make your brush drier, press the heel (not the tip, which would draw off the color) to your paper towel or cloth before you touch the brush to the stone. This will allow excess moisture to drain from the fibers.

It is convenient to have the black sumi available on a flat surface, such as the grinding face of the ink stone or on a plate. You want only a touch or a small quantity of the dark ink on the side of the brush. If you attempt to get this ink from the comparatively deep well of ink at the foot of the suzuri, no matter how careful you are you will find your brush absorbing too much ink. It also takes time to be so careful. With the ink on a flat surface, you can more precisely control the amount and location of the dark ink.

The result of adding this touch of dark ink to each brushload will be lines and strokes that inevitably speak more eloquently, if only by contrast. There will always be a touch or edge of darker ink bringing out the true tone, i.e., the color, of each line and stroke.

ON THE USE OF COLOR

While color can be added to sumi-e, it is generally applied with moderation. Experimenting with color can strongly inform the sense of tone and shading inherent in your use of black and white. Color is also attractive in its own right, of course. And you will want to test its effects in combination with sumi.

The colors you use should be color-fast, which means they won't run when re-wet. Since rice paper must be lined with a wet method, it is essential to use watercolors containing glue. Winsor Newton artist colors are excellent for use with sumi. The colors are brighter, however, than Japanese colors. They are most appropriate for haiga-style paintings (combining poetry and painting), Chinese-style paintings, and for filling in sumi outlines with color.

You may want to use Japanese watercolors (tablets) or Chinese watercolors (tubes). Be sure whatever you buy is not made for Western-style watercoloring as some of these have no glue. The best, least expensive colors for use with sumi are those imported by Boku-undo, called *kansai.* They are small, dime-sized tablets of finely ground and subtle color, especially designed for use with sumi. The cakes are hard, however, and require some effort with the brush to work up a strong color. What gives these colors body is that they are applied after being mixed with a touch of sumi on the brush. At this writing, a set of 12 colors costs $6.50.

Color works best with sumi when the two are mixed on the same brush. If you look at the cover of this book, you will see that sumi is mixed with many of the strokes. The color in the cover art, incidentally, is somewhat stronger than the "touch" of color that would be found in traditional sumi painting.

Sumi is mixed with color in three ways: 1) a base of grey can be loaded onto the brush and colors added at the tip or sides;   2) color is put on the brush and dark or medium sumi is added at the tip or sides;   3) color is put on the brush and sumi is added on one side and another color on the opposite side or tip. While I have broken color mixing into three types, there are many variations you may wish to try.

Colors work best when mixed, blended and combined on one brush. If a scene of trees has colors of light green, dark green, blue, and brown, work them all on the same brushload along with some sumi. Let your brush choose where to lay down the colors. You need not paint each color separately. To do so may mean losing some of the spontaneity in your tone and shading.

Free choice of coloration is also important in developing your own color sense. Color is in the eye of the beholder, and it is also at the choice of the beholder. Don't be concerned if the colors in your box of paints do not match the scene you are painting. A flower has many shades, tones and colors and your color instinct may choose to emphasize the truth of a particular sub-modality of tone or color. Refer to what is out there in nature, but trust to the truth of your own senses.

Traditional Japanese sumi-e allows only touches of color. But for you and me, there are no rules except those that we discover work best in our own painting exploration. If you like color, use it to the degree that is appropriate for your own satisfaction.

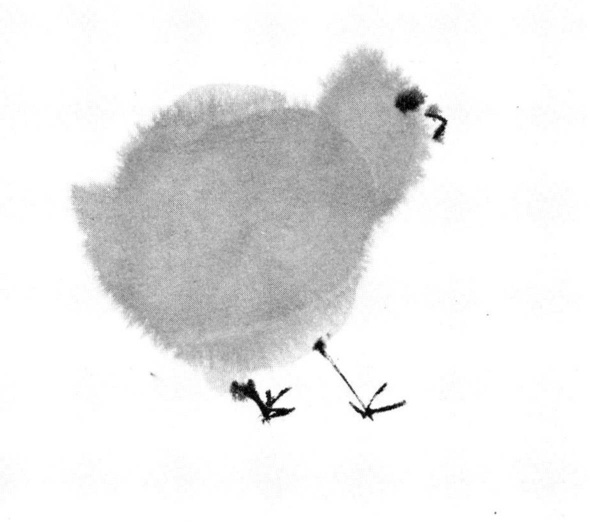

Fuzzy Chick. Not much color here. But then, the parts of a chick that stand out from the fur are the legs, eyes and beak.

LINING THE PAINTINGS

It is necessary to line your paintings before they can be matted or framed. Rice paper is very thin and the water used in this type of painting causes the paper to wrinkle. The process of lining removes the wrinkles, flattens and strengthens the painting, and also brings out the tones more strongly. Most picture framers do not know how to do lining, so you will have to learn to do it yourself. It is relatively simple, however, once you get the idea. Practice first on less important paintings.

Lining basically involves wetting and stretching the entire painting, glueing another piece of rice paper to the back, and glueing the four sides to a board so the painting will be stretched evenly and will dry wrinkle-free. The process is similar to stretching a fabric or tightening a drum.

The materials you will need for lining are:

1. A flat, hard, nonporous surface — glass, marble, formica or plastic — at least 4" larger on each side than the largest painting you plan to line. A glass or marble-topped table, a mirror, or a kitchen counter can serve the purpose. I use a large piece of plate glass.

2. Glue. Cornstarch is fine and is even used by major museums. You will also need alum, purchased in any drugstore, to keep bugs from eating the starch.

3. Lining paper. Rice paper of medium weight, not too light and not too heavy. Taiwan cotton, Suzuki, or the long rolls are all good. The paper must be larger than the painting you wish to line by 2" on a side. Optional is a cardboard tube, such as a mailing tube, longer than the width of the lining paper.

4. A spray bottle of water, such as for misting plants, to dampen the painting and stretch it.

5. A wide, short-haired, soft-bristled "water brush," such as a hake (see pg.83, figure 37, brush 7c) for smoothing the damp painting.

6. A foam brush, sponge, or wide, short-haired, soft-bristled brush (a hake will do in a pinch) for applying glue to the back of the painting. If you use a sponge, dampen it first; otherwise the moisture will be drawn from the glue. I find that the foam brushes mounted on handles, generally used to paint walls, work very well.

7. A large "smoothing brush" for smoothing the lining paper onto the back of the painting, such as a *soft-bristled* whisk broom, a wallpaper glue brush, or a 4"-wide paintbrush with bristles cut down to 1-1/2" or 2". The brush should be firm but not so stiff that it scrapes fibers off the lining paper surface, particularly if the lining paper has been dampened first.

8. Lining board. This is a clean board large enough to hold the mounted work, either 4'x4' or 4'x8'. A 3/8"- or 1/2"-thick plywood or a 1/4"-thick Masonite board will do.

9. Other materials. A pot or bowl to hold the glue, something to boil water, a sponge and bowl for clean water to clean the glass, and paper towels or cloths for wiping the glass clean and dry. Later, you will need a mat knife to cut the painting off the board and perhaps scissors to trim the painting.

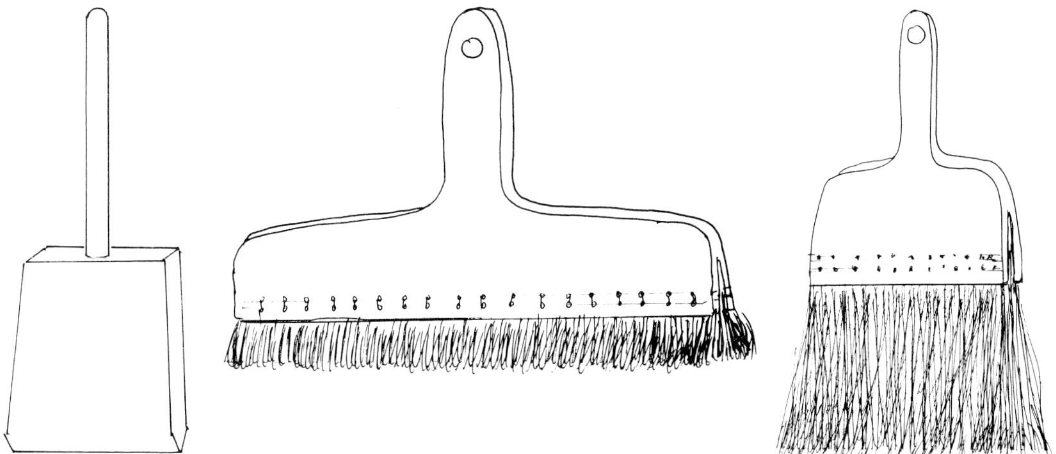

A 'foam' brush (left) can be used to apply glue. A Japanese paste brush (center) can also be used. For smoothing out wrinkles, use a Japanese smoothing brush (right).

The Lining Process

The first step in lining is to make the glue. Glue must be used warm, so prepare it just before you begin. Depending on how large your paintings are, the proportions for 5 or 6 paintings are 1 tablespoon cornstarch, a pinch of alum, and a cup of water; for 10 to 20 paintings, use 1/4 cup cornstarch, 2 pinches of alum, and one quart of water. Put the starch and alum in a bowl, or enamel pot (not aluminum), add enough cold water to make a thick liquid, and pour in the rapidly boiling water while stirring.

Next, measure a piece of lining paper 2" to 3" larger all around than the painting. Dampen the paper by spraying *very lightly* with water. Then roll the paper onto the cardboard tube and set aside.

Place the painting face-down on the lining surface, and mist lightly until damp. The paper will begin to stretch as it absorbs the water. Don't overwet the painting. Gently smooth out air bubbles and wrinkles with the slightly damp water brush. Brush from the center out, carefully lifting corners if necessary to get our wrinkles.

Next apply an even coat of glue, brushing from the center out. The painting will continue to stretch. If wrinkles and air bubbles appear, you may have to gently lift

Whether applying glue or smoothing out wrinkles and air bubbles, brush from the center out.

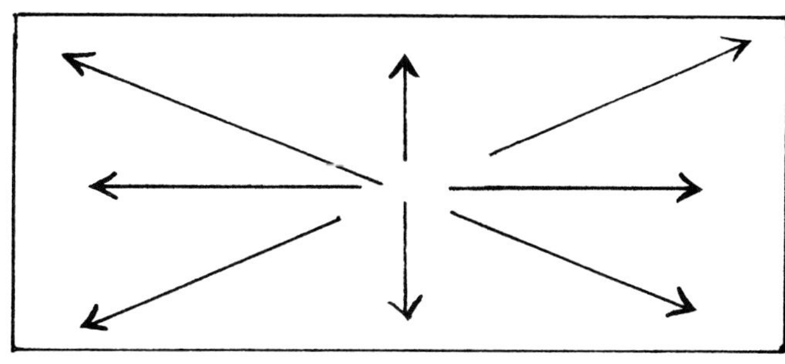

the corners to smooth them out. Be careful, because the wet painting tears easily. Don't try to get out every wrinkle or tiny air bubble. Use enough glue to thoroughly moisten and cover the back of the painting, then brush across the entire painting in long strokes to even out the glue.

Use a damp sponge to carefully but quickly clean the glue that has gotten on the lining surface around the sides of the painting and dry the surface.

The next step is to brush the lining paper onto the glued back of the painting. Place the tube of lining paper on the glass about 2" from one end of the painting. Carefully align the tube so that when the lining paper is unrolled, it will cover the painting. As you slowly unroll the lining paper over the painting, gently brush back and forth with the smoothing brush. The purpose is to guarantee the adhesion of the two papers. Do not brush too vigorously or the dampened lining paper will tear or shred.

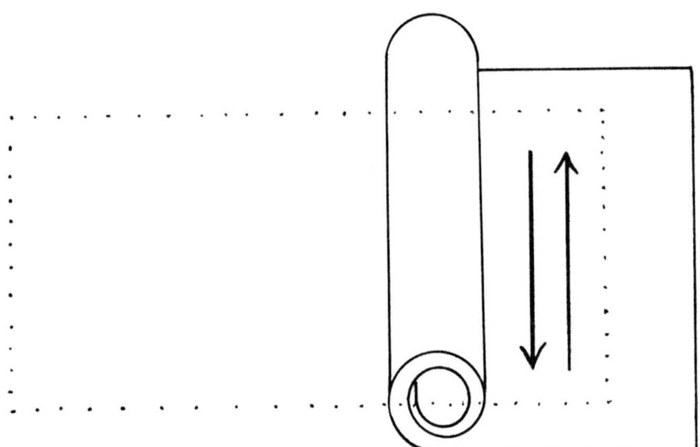

While one hand slowly unrolls the lining paper, apply back-and-forth brush strokes, from edge to edge, with the other hand.

The glued painting will show through the lining paper as the moisture penetrates it. When it is all down, brush back and forth to make sure there are no "white spots" where the two pieces fail to adhere, especially at the edges of the painting.

The next step is to put a border of glue around the circumference of the painting. This will allow you to glue the painting to the lining board. Don't drip glue on the painting.

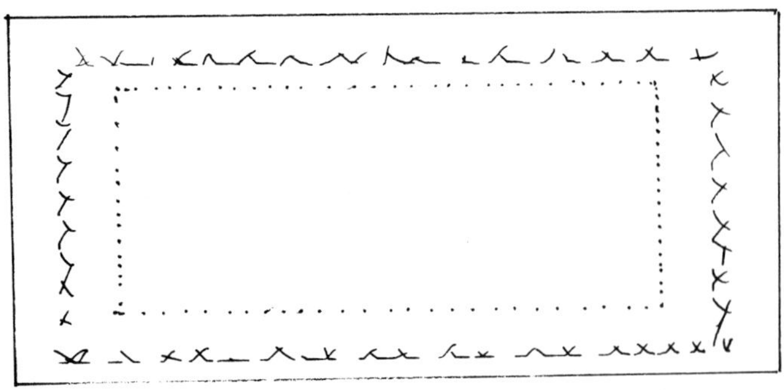

Put a glue border on the lining paper outside the perimeter of the painting.

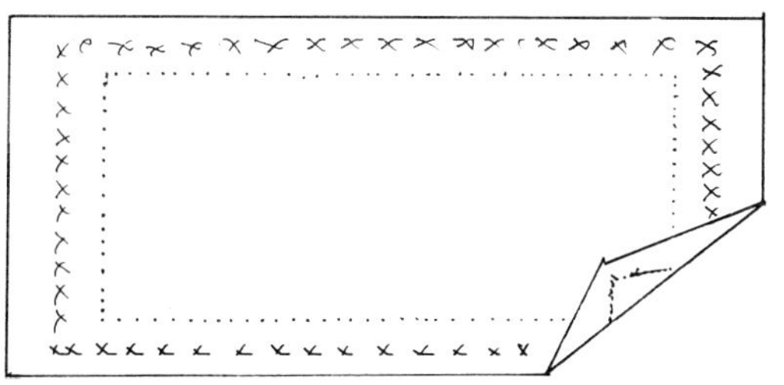

Make sure the painting adheres to the lining paper.

Starting at one corner, carefully lift a tiny section of the lining paper to make sure the painting adheres to the lining paper and doesn't stick to the lining surface. If the papers begin to separate from each other at the corner, use your fingernail or a sharp tool to break the adherence to the lining surface. Then slowly lift the entire lined painting away from the surface. You will want to get your fingers on the inside of the glue border to prevent the weight of the wet painting from ripping the glued edge. Attach the painting to the lining board, starting at the top, then the bottom, then the sides. Make sure the painting is attached all around by brushing the glued circumference outwards with the backs of your fingernails or with the smoothing brush. Don't brush the painting itself, only the glued edges.

Clean your lining surface and you're ready to do the next lining.

Lined paintings usually may be removed the next day, when they are completely dry. Cut carefully around the edge of the painting with the mat knife, remove from the board, and trim the edges with scissors. You can also trim the painting using a straight edge and the mat knife. The painting is now ready for matting and framing.

All materials can be easily cleaned using warm water containing a small amount of liquid dish soap.

Bamboo Landscape.

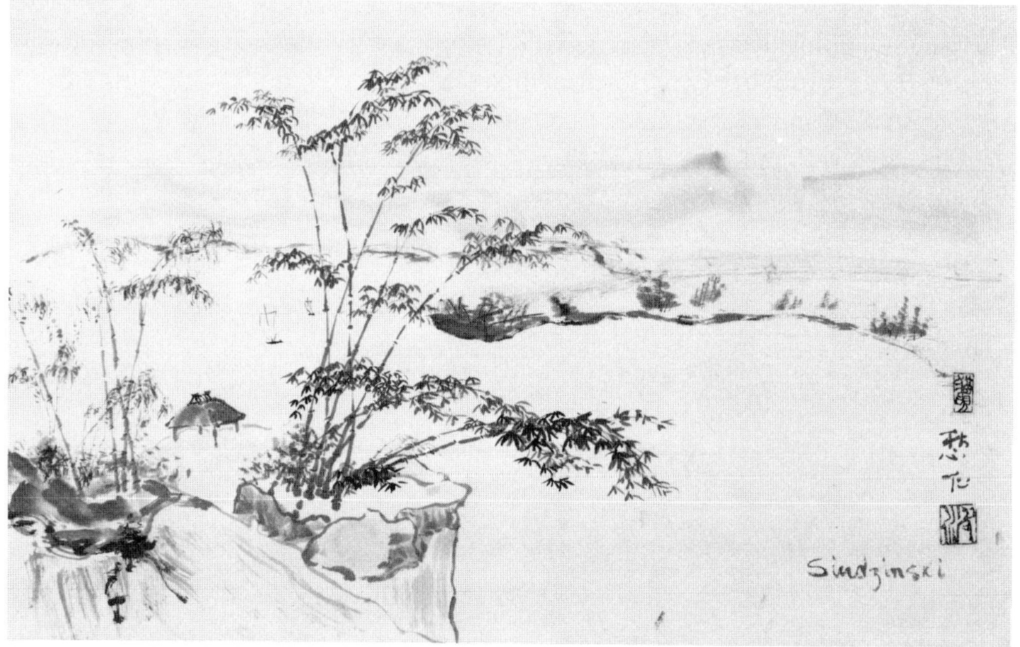

Many schools of sumi-e have been formed around, or initiated by, a particular artist. Many artists teach in their homes or at local schools. Check with community centers, colleges, and adult education programs. A list of teachers is available from the Sumi-e Society of America. Write to SUMI-E, c/o Betzi Robinson, 7102 Westbury Road, McLean, VA 22101.

Some of the following teachers give instruction in Chinese or Oriental rather than Japanese ink painting. They can, however, generally provide a good introduction to the brush arts. In choosing a teacher and in studying meditative painting, be alert to the spirit in which the art is practiced rather than the name by which it is known.

SCHOOLS IN NORTH AMERICA:

Lassie Corbett, 2305 Acton Drive, Reston, VA 22091
Wo Yue-Kee (Henry Wo), 8325 Fleetwood Ct., Alexandria, VA 22308
I-Hsiung Ju, The Art Farm, Rt. 5, Box 85, Lexington, VA 24450
Grace Braley, 123 Indian Lane, Annapolis, MD 21403
Ming Friedman, 8106 Accotink St., Annandale, VA 22003
Marion Ott, 7310 Elgar St., Springfield, VA 22151
Kawai Sumi-e Workshop, Japan Cultural Center, 313½ East First Street, Los Angeles, CA 90012
Kaji Aso Studio, 40 St. Stephen St., Boston, MA 02109
Koho School of Sumi-e, 64 MacDougal St., New York, NY 10014
Motoi Oi, Oi School, 24-50 95th St., East Elmhurst, NY 11369 (correspondence course)
Mitsuko Bickman, 19 Kime Ave., North Babylon, NY 11703
Paul Reps, 2225 12th Ave. E., Seattle, WA 98102 (Zen Art)
TAO Art, P.O. Box 58630, Dallas, TX 75258

A School of Fish.

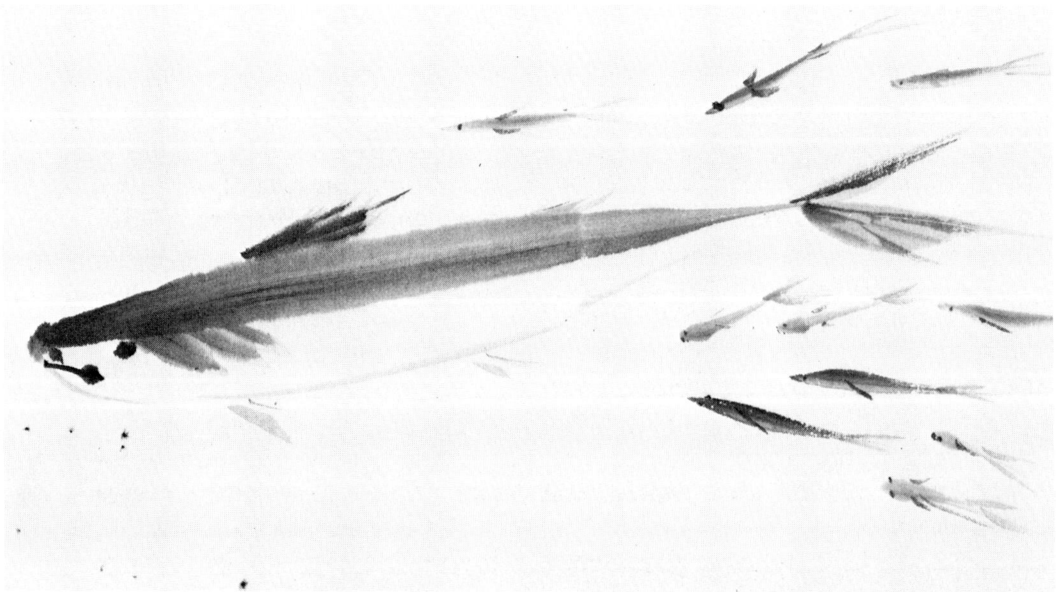

Susan Link, RFD 293, East Lake Road, Fitzwilliam, NH 03447
Elaine Campbell, RR1, Angus Dr., Westbank, B.C., Canada V0H 2A0
Werner Sperling, 400 N. Eighth St., Stroudsburg, PA 18360
Glory Brightfield, Box 23, Bearsville, NY 12409
Ed Nelson, Phoenix Workshop at Sharon Arts Center, RFD 1, Goffstown, NH 03045 (summer only)
Miyoko Moody, 409 Dahlia St., Biloxi, MS 39531
Kazuko Reynolds, 2222 Ledgeview Lane, Spring Valley, CA 92077
Kay Thomas, 253 Oak Knoll Terrace, Highland Park, IL 60035
Roppei Matsumoto, 41 Linnaean St., Cambridge, MA 02138
Barbara Hiestrand, P.O. Box 57, Bolinas, CA 94924
Dorothy Radyk, 3155 Hacienda St., San Mateo, CA 94403
Fumiko Kimura, 1615 Frilands Dr., Tacoma, WA 89405
Vivian O'Brien, 9595 Parktane, Plantation, FL 33324
David Donar, 12970 W. Virginia St., Lakewood. CO 80220
Mona Coman, Salisbury Cove, Sand Point Rd., Bar Harbor, ME 04609
Lucy Liu, 11513 Palatine Ave., Seattle, WA 98133
Marjorie Newman, 553 Highland Ave., Sheridan, WY 82801
Edythe Newbourne, Box 5112, Dearborn Heights, MI 48128
Cheng Khee Chee, 1508 Vermillion Road, Duluth, MN 55812
Betty Mighton, 711 Ambleside Drive, Wilmington, DE 19808
Marie Shaughnessy, 1419 Annapolis Drive, Anchorage, AK 99504
Jan Applebaum, 151 Bay St., Suite 1006, Ottawa, Ontario, Canada K1R 7T2
Betty Sanjek, 16 Spruce Road, Larchmont, NY 10538
Ellen Vartanoff, 6825 Wilson Lane, Bethesda, MD 20030
Japanese Canadian Cultural Center, 123 Wynford Dr., Don Mills, Toronto, Ont., Canada
Sharon Nakazato, 83–74 116th St., Richmond Hill, NY 11418 (Japanese Calligraphy)
A Meditation in Ink, 80 Norwood Road, Northport, NY 11768
   (Inquiries concerning this book may also be sent to this address.)

SUPPLIES

One of the biggest and best art supply houses in Japan is Gyokusen-do. They will be able to fill your orders for brushes, paper, ink, and so on. They do not have an English catalog, so you will have to know what you want to some extent. If you know someone who reads Japanese, he or she may order for you from the catalog or write the letter for you in Japanese. The address is: Gyokusen-do, Kanda Jimbocho, 3-3, Chiyoda-ku, Tokyo, Japan 101.

Another quality supplier is: Saiundo Fujimoto, Anekoji Fuyacho Higashi, Nakagyo-ku, Kyoto, Japan 604. Also: Kyukuodo, Anekojikado, Teramachi-cho, Chukyo-ku, Kyoto has an excellent selection of brushes and other supplies, but they do not ship. Buy when you visit Japan!

When writing to Japan, it is wise to include self-addressed mailing labels.

In America, the biggest wholesale importer is Yasutomo. If you write to them, they will tell you the address of the nearest retail outlet. They stock a variety of brushes, ink, paper, and other items. The address is: Yasutomo & Company, 24 California St., San Francisco, CA 94111. Another good importer, located in New York, who will also do mail order is: Boku-undo, 110 Greene St., New York, NY 10012.

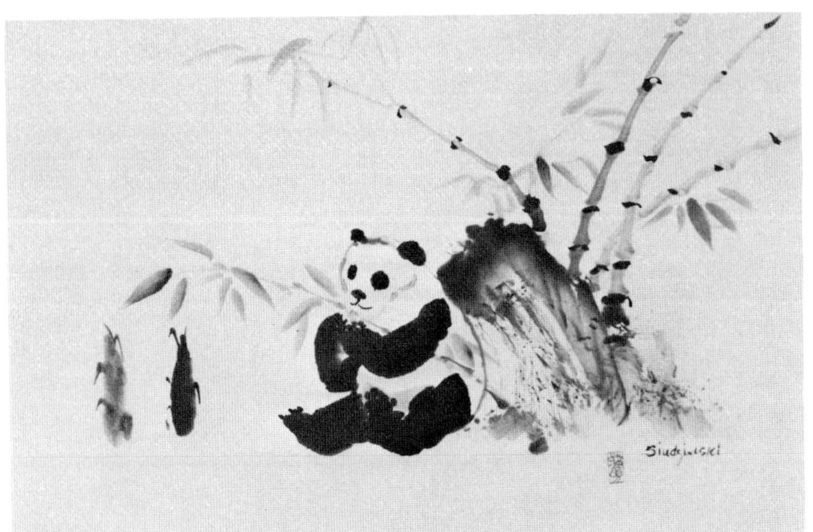

Bamboo Breakfast. Pandas are a natural subject for black and white, but then so is bamboo.

Most Japanese stores, many Chinese stationery stores, and some specialty stores carry Oriental art materials. In New York try one of the Azumas, or the Zen Oriental Book Store, 521 Fifth Ave., New York, NY 10017. In San Francisco, try Honami or Kinokuniya in the Japan Trade Center or Cando K. Hoshino's Art Supplies, 1541 Clement St., San Francisco, CA 94618.

Mail order houses include:

Aiko's Art Materials, 714 N. Wabash Ave., Dept. B. Chicago, IL 60611
    (catalog $.75 sample pack of rice paper $8.25)
Guy T. Kuhn, 31 S. Potomac St., Hagerstown, MD 21740 (rice papers, list and sample pack $5)
Oriental Art Supplies, 135 Fort Williams Pkwy., Alexandria, VA 22304 (Chinese materials)

Other suppliers:

H.R. Meininger Co., 1415 Tremont Pl., Denver, CO 80202
China Cultural Center, 970 North Broadway No. 210, Los Angeles, CA 90012 (catalog)
Art and Things, Inc., 2 Annapolis St., Annapolis, MD 21401
Back Room Art Supplies, New London, NH 03257
Hakubundo, Inc., 100 N. Beretania St., Honolulu, HI 96817
Chinese Cultural Service, 123 N. 10th St., Philadelphia, PA 19107

Art supply stores sometimes carry inexpensive Oriental painting supplies, as does Pearl Paint Co., 308 Canal St., New York, NY 10010. Try the largest art supply dealer in your area, or the art and book store of a local university or art school.

A list of Oriental "rice papers" and their qualities can be found in *The How and Why of Chinese Painting* by Diana Kan (Van Nostrand Reinhold).

Seals can be ordered from Japan or they can be carved in this country by native Japanese or Chinese seal carvers. If you are ordering from Japan you may ask Gyokusen-do, the art supply house in Tokyo, to recommend a seal carver for you. Or perhaps you know someone who has ordered from a carver they know in Japan. In America you are most likely to contact a seal carver through an Oriental art supply dealer, through a local art league, or through an artist who works in the Oriental style. If you are in New York, you may order Chinese seals from Yue-San Kan, 75 East End Ave., New York, NY 10028 and Japanese seals from Sharon Nakazato, 83—74 116th St., Richmond Hill, NY 11418. An excellent supplier of most things, including seals and inexpensive scrolls, is the Art Farm, Rt. 5, Box 85, Lexington, VA 24450.

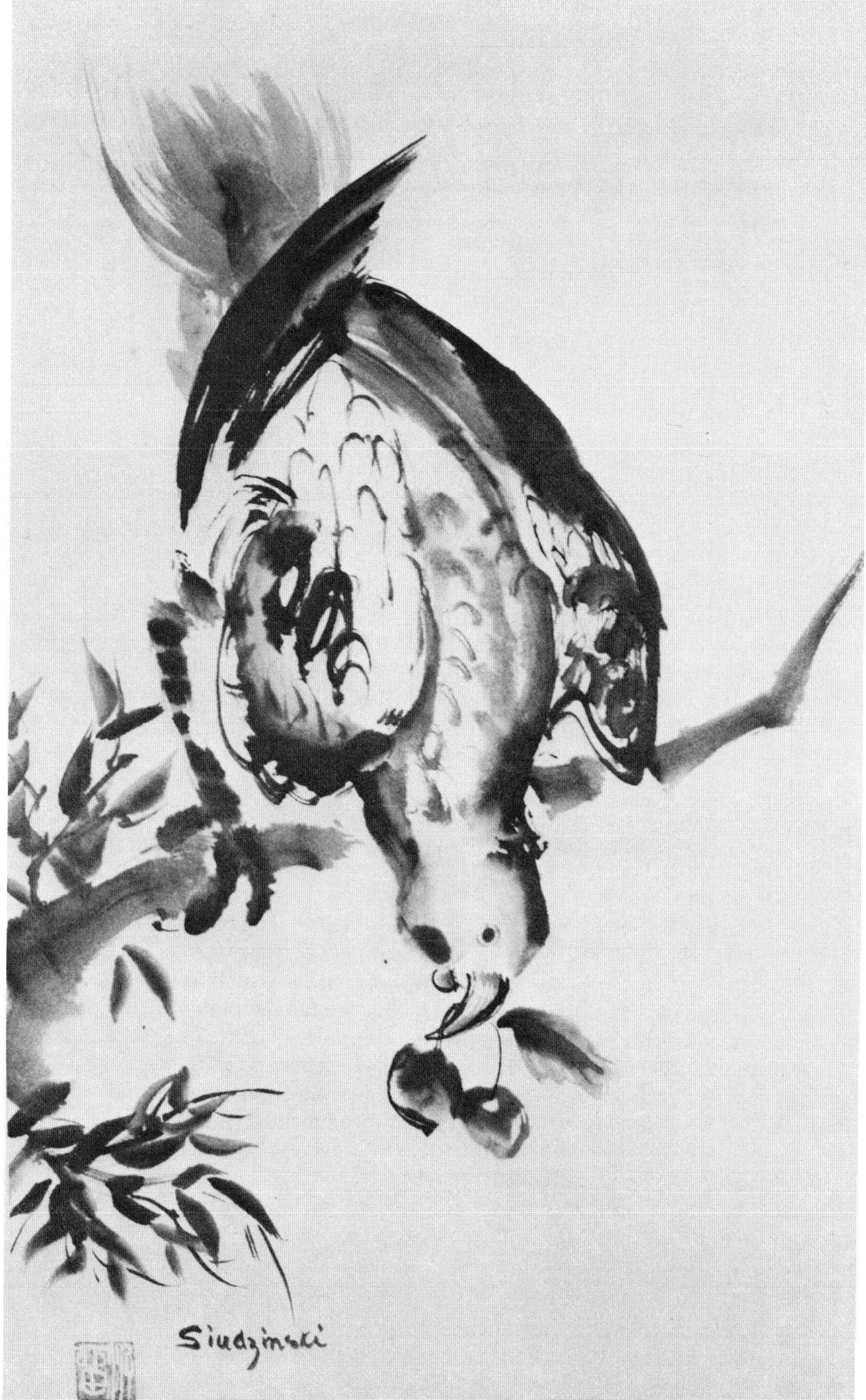

Siudzinski

A NOTE ON THE MEDITATIONS

The principle behind the meditative approach to painting, and the reason it works, is that it lulls the logical, critical, dominant part of the mind to sleep while allowing the creative, curious, and spatially perceptive part to surface. The concept is similar to that explicated by Betty Edwards in her book, *Drawing on the Right Side of the Brain,* and is also seminal to Frederick Franck's *The Zen of Seeing.*

The existence of this left brain/right brain dichotomy is the rationale behind the music I always play during my classes. I find that music invokes a mode of nonlinear perception similar to the mental "understanding" involved with the activity of painting.

Perhaps you have had the experience of putting on a tape or recording of a piece of music you wanted to listen to and then becoming so involved with something else — knitting, daydreaming, reading; visual activities are particularly susceptible — that you "forget" to listen. Sometime later, you notice the music has stopped. Where were you during the interim? Perhaps visiting your right brain, creating pictures and visions for your artistic self.

Playing music in my painting classes — generally Japanese flute music or other quiet music that doesn't demand attention — serves to amplify or reinforce the right brain mode. In other words, I have found that music supports our serious, curious, playful painter.

Freeing the creative self is an ongoing process that can take you as deeply as you want to go into your own artistic nature. And of course, the student wants guidance, reassurance, that one can trust the creative process to provide a personal roadmap marked by surprise, delight, and new learning. Ultimately, barriers and problems become opportunities for further growth.

Thus, a second, equally important aspect of meditative painting is to assist the student in drawing upon his or her own resources when learning new lessons or meeting barriers so as to be able to transform them into new opportunities. The meditations I now conduct in my classes are designed to introduce students to their own unique resources, their inner guides, and to help point the way toward future encounters and successes.

These meditations are beyond the scope of the present volume. They form a series, each linked to the others, with numerous aspects that require substantial detail. This meditative process will be the subject of my next book.

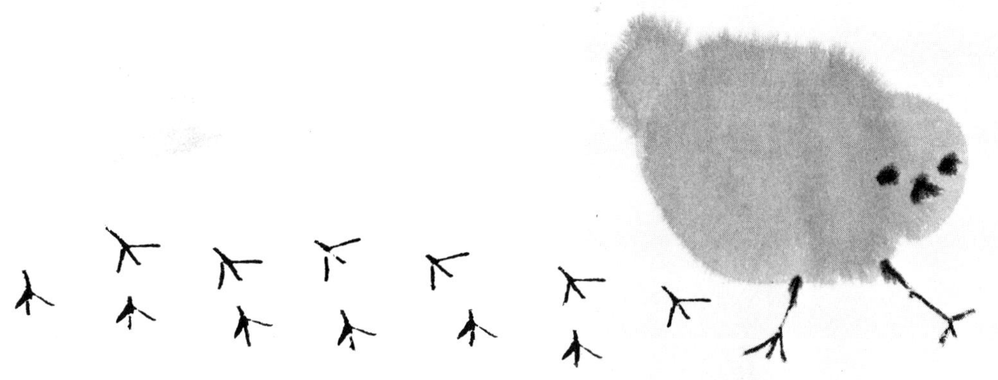